RAILWAYS AROUI
LAKE LUZERN

Martin Bairstow

11502 'Nyon' pulls into Brunnen with a northbound semi fast on 1 September 1987.   *(Martin Bairstow)*

Published by Martin Bairstow, Fountain Chambers, Halifax, West Yorkshire
Printed by Amadeus Press Ltd, Huddersfield, West Yorkshire

Introduction

I am grateful to Geoffrey Lewthwaite for loaning me his original first edition copy of *Switzerland's Amazing Railways* by Cecil J. Allen. Published in 1953, this is something of a classic in railway literature. The word 'amazing' was probably chosen to emphasise the contrast between the railways of Switzerland and those with which Mr Allen was even more familiar closer to home.

Cecil J. Allen was a student of locomotive performance. For over 60 years, first in the *Railway Magazine* and more latterly in *Modern Railways* he described each month the exploits of loco crews battling against such mountainous obstacles as 'The Long Drag', the 17 mile climb from Settle Junction at 1 in 100. What a contrast it must have been to experience the electric locos in Switzerland sailing up gradients steeper than 1 in 40 seemingly without effort.

There were many other amazing features of Swiss Railways starting perhaps with the fact that they were built at all – the way they conquered difficult terrain with their spiral tunnels, rack and pinion sections – the way they gave such reliable service even in weather far more adverse than anything we experience in our own country.

Then there was the way that, even in the early 1950s, the Swiss Railways were seen as part of an overall transport system. Our own Government had recently nationalised not just the railways but most road transport and vested it all in the totally unwieldy British Transport Commission with a remit to integrate the various modes – but they never did. The Swiss by contrast were happy to leave the trains, buses, ships and cable cars in a variety of different ownerships – all dedicated to providing one integrated service. The 1953 book describes some of the efforts being made even then to foster use of public transport including the half fare pass. Charge the passenger an up front fee with half fare thereafter. Once he's bought his card he has the incentive to travel. Just like the motorist who has taxed and insured his car.

There is perhaps another amazing feature of Cecil J Allen's book which he may not have foreseen in 1953. That is the extent to which his narrative is still relevant and recognisable today.

In most countries, not least our own, the railway scene of the late 1990s would bear little semblance to that of the early fifties. But in Switzerland, there has been no closure of half the network. There has been no modernisation plan. They didn't need one because they had not allowed development to fall behind. There have been no periodic reorganisations.

The principal main line companies were nationalised in 1902 to create the Swiss Federal Railways (Schweizerische Bundesbahnen). There was provision for the SBB to take over other railways which it did, principally in 1909, when it absorbed the Gotthard Bahn, the main north – south

Trans Alpine Railway. After that the SBB made very few acquisitions leaving it in control of just under 60% of the total route mileage. The remainder is in the hands of over 100 different organisations: the Privatbahnen. But 'privat' should translate as 'non Federal'. It certainly does not mean 'privatised'. Many of the lines are owned in whole or in part by the Cantons. They vary in size from the important Rhätischen Bahn and the Bern – Lötschberg – Simplon to the tiniest funiculars.

When Cecil J. Allen went from Luzern to St Gallen, he explained that for 38 km between Arth Goldau and Rapperswil he was travelling on the Sud Ost Bahn. That is still the case today but it doesn't prevent them from running through services. At Göschenen, on the Gotthard Main line, he changed onto a branch of the Furka Oberalp. When he took the Brünig line all the way to Interlaken Ost, he encountered the brown locomotives of the Bern – Lötschberg – Simplon and the narrow gauge stock of the Berner Oberland Bahn. Just like today.

But this is not to say that nothing has changed during 4½ decades. Against a background of stability, there has been an almost constant process of evolution. The trains have become more frequent, particularly with the introduction of the Taktfahrplan in 1982 (the nationwide regular interval timetable). They have certainly become more comfortable. Efforts have continued to boost traffic: the half fare card, free travel for accompanied children, facilities for tourists. The railways have been taken direct into the Airport terminals at Zürich and Geneva. There is the fly luggage. There is the promise of new Alpine tunnels.

In this book, we look at the railways in the very heart of Switzerland, in the area around Lake Luzern. There are main lines and branch lines, standard and narrow gauge. There are rack lines, one as steep as 1 in 2, and funiculars even steeper than that. There is not a lot of steam – except on the lake itself but there is practically everything else that one could hope to find on a railway system. And it all works to a very high standard.

I would like to thank everybody who has helped. Glynis Boocock somehow typed the manuscript from my scribble. Geoffrey Lewthwaite loaned some of the tickets. The photographs are credited individually. John Holroyd drew the gradient profiles. I drew the maps.

It is hoped that the book will serve as an introduction and guide to the railways of Central Switzerland, maybe helping visitors to get more out of their trip or possibly tempting others to go for the first time.

Gute Reise!

Halifax, West Yorkshire
April 1997   Martin Bairstow

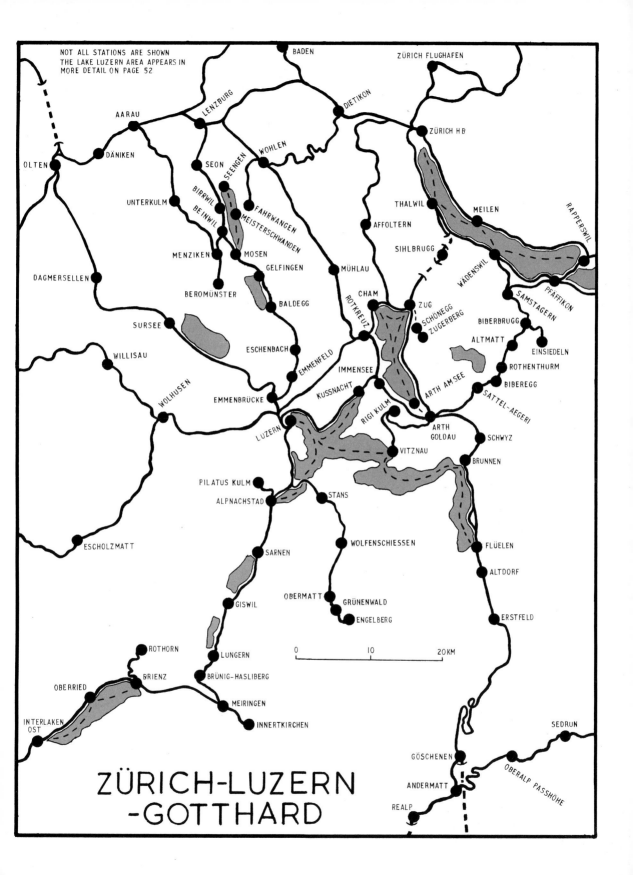

NOT ALL STATIONS ARE SHOWN
THE LAKE LUZERN AREA APPEARS IN
MORE DETAIL ON PAGE 52

ZÜRICH-LUZERN -GOTTHARD

Getting away from it all

Monday 15 August 1994, Halifax. We are in the middle of the Railtrack signalling dispute. Not for the first time, we are watching the British railway industry hell bent on destroying itself. Hardly a pleasant sight for someone who has taken so deep an interest in the subject this last 30 odd years.

Today is a strike day but we have an emergency rail service for getting home. I shall have to leave work a little early because tonight I am booked to give a slide show in Ilkley on the subject of *Railways in the Austrian Tirol*. I go for the 16.41 train from Halifax to New Pudsey. It is 23 minutes late. When I get home it is a mad rush to grab a bite to eat and load the car with everything I need for the slide show.

Tuesday 16 August, another strike day. The emergency timetable functions well today.

Wednesday 17 August, 'normal service'. I really could do with getting home on time as we have a very early start tomorrow when we set off for Switzerland. I stay at work to try and tidy up but am out of Fountain Chambers at ten past six. With luck I may get the 18.18, failing which it will have to be the 18.33. Why did I rush? The 18.18 is 27 minutes late and the 18.33 no better. When I was younger, I could have cycled home quicker.

In *Railways in the Bernese Oberland* I described the rail/sea journey all the way from New Pudsey to Interlaken West. I seem to recall BR almost failing at the first hurdle and wrecking our travel plans on that occasion.

The trip in 1986 was the last I made by that particular method. Five subsequent expeditions to Switzerland have all been by air using scheduled flights booked as a package with accommodation through Kuoni.

The Swissair flight leaves Manchester each morning at 7.45. We had planned to get to the Airport by booking a taxi for 3.45 in order to catch the 4.21 train from Leeds. These night trains are a bit slow as they are allowed 30 minutes recovery time for engineering works etc but it isn't that which has put us off. We have been blighted by the strikes. As it happens neither our outward nor return journeys are on actual strike days but we didn't know that when we made our revised plans.

So those ardent railway supporters, Martin Bairstow and Philippa Simpson plus eight year old Stephen set out at 4.45am (one hour later note) by car for Littleborough. Here we pick up our friend Stuart Carmichael who kindly drives us to Manchester Airport and will then keep our car at Littleborough for the duration of the trip.

In contrast to recent flights on charter aircraft, our Swissair McDonnell Douglas 81 has plenty of leg room even in economy class. It is away from the terminal at exactly 7.45. During the 90 minute flight we are served with free breakfast, a newspaper to remind us of the continuing deadlock in the Railtrack dispute, a colouring book for my son and the inevitable inflight magazine. Here perhaps is the first hint that we are going somewhere different. Inside this rather non-technical general interest publication is a map of Switzerland – in colour. Had this been a British map one might expect to find the motorways in thick blue lines, the major roads in red and the railways, if they are shown at all, in very thin black lines. But not this time. The red lines are the railways. The 'autobahnen' are white and far less prominent.

The area around the map gives details of various rail/public transport facilities in Switzerland including a reminder that Zürich and Geneva Airports are directly rail-served with minimum connection times of 40 minutes plane to train and 60 minutes the other way round.

We are on the ground at 10.15 (having of course advanced our watches one hour). A bus takes us from the plane to the terminal where passports and Customs formalities are minimal.

The only slight delay is in waiting for Stephen's suitcase to come along the conveyor belt. Since he isn't paying any fares in Switzerland (of which more anon), he hasn't been issued with a 'Fly Luggage' label which is part of our inclusive deal. But for this, we might just have caught the 10.42 train to Zürich Hauptbahnhof which would have had us in Brunnen at 12.04.

Outside Switzerland, the majority of package tour operators convey you from airport to holiday destination by bus. Rail transfers are comparatively rare and usually found only on expensive specialist holidays. In Switzerland, rail transfers are the norm.

In entrusting patrons to the 'Swiss Travel System', tour operators are relying on four vital factors:
(1) The consistent reliability of the Swiss Railways and other transport operators.
(2) Main line stations underneath the airports at Zürich and Geneva.
(3) The Fly Luggage System.
(4) Special fare deals such as the Swiss Card described later.

So having retrieved my son's suitcase, we make our way through the terminal in the direction of the underground railway station. Pausing only to purchase a timetable, we are in plenty of time for the 11.05 departure. We take our seats in an air-conditioned carriage belonging to the Bern – Lötschberg – Simplon Railway – an immediate reminder that there are several main line railway companies in Switzerland. This coach is well endowed with leg room. The Swiss appear not yet to have learnt how to cram extra seats into their trains. They still follow the practice of having a block of four seats to each window with space for luggage both on overhead racks and between the seat backs. Thanks to its length, each carriage has 88 seats plus a loo. Each seating bay has a small table with map of the BLS on the top and litter bin underneath. The train is going to Brig but we are only on it for 13 minutes to Zürich Hauptbahnhof.

Opened in 1981, the four platform station at Zürich Flughafen lies part way through a 4 km long

Four days and four hours after our journey, 11605 'Uster' is ready to leave Zürich Hauptbahnhof with the 16.05 to Chiasso via the Gotthard Main Line. The train has reversed at Zürich following arrival from Schaffhausen.
(Martin Bairstow)

tunnel which forms a loop off the original Winterthur to Zürich route. In the normal hourly sequence there are five trains into Zürich Hauptbahnhof but this is not just an airport shuttle service. The 10.42 which we might have caught was an 'Inter City' through from St Gallen in the north east of Switzerland to Genève Aeroport in the extreme south west. The train we have caught starts at Zürich Flughafen and is going via the capital, Bern, all the way to Brig near the entrance to the Simplon Tunnel which leads into Italy.

Our first and only intermediate stop is reached after 6 minutes at Oerlikon, a name which appears on the builder's plates of many Swiss carriages. We have left the Airport tunnel and have already joined three other routes converging on Zürich. Outside the station building to our left are the distinctive blue trams which operate a dense network in and around the City.

In terms of population, Zürich is the largest of the 23 Swiss Cantons with just over one million inhabitants. To put it into perspective, it is much smaller than West Yorkshire or Greater Manchester but public transport, and in particular rail facilities, are on a radically different scale.

As we approach Zürich Hauptbahnhof, there is a vast expanse of tracks on either side. We see a train of Austrian carriages forming the Euro City 'Maria Theresia' upon which we travelled last year between St Anton and Innsbruck whilst preparing *Railways in the Austrian Tirol*. Somewhat in contrast is the short low level TALGO stock which will be working the 'Hotelzug Pablo Casals' overnight to Madrid. All around are the suburban trains including the double deck push-pull formations diving down towards the underground 'S-bahn' platforms.

There are 18 platforms in the main terminal part of the station to which are added those in the two underground sections: the S-Bahn at the north end

and the Uetliberg suburban mountain line which is found underneath the south end of the concourse. There is also the tram terminal outside.

The moment our train screeches to a halt, it is attacked at both ends by shunters with protective helmets, one at the buffer stop end to detach the locomotive which has brought us in and the other to prepare the drawgear, brake and power connections at the rear in readiness to couple on the loco which will take the train forward to Bern.

We venture outside the great portico passing under the tramway station and main road to reach Bahnhofstrasse, pedestrianised, apart from trams, which extends down to the lake. We contemplate walking to the lake, returning by tram but settle instead for coffee at McDonalds.

Our train at 12.03, is through from Schaffhausen to Chiasso. The carriages are in the traditional dark green livery but with a blue band just below the waist line. This indicates that they have been refurbished with upholstered seating replacing the previous plastic covers.

The open interior is spacious if a little spartan. It is also functional and easy to clean. It is not air conditioned except by the time honoured method of lowering the windows right down. Travelling in warm weather can be quite a breezy affair.

Our 60 minute journey begins with a long curve which takes us through almost 180 degrees. Leaving Zürich Hauptbahnhof we were facing north west but as we pass through Enge Station, our direction is south east. We are now alongside Lake Zürich. Passing Wollishofen, we catch a fleeting glimpse of a paddle steamer, a form of transport which will feature quite prominently in our holiday and also in this book. Our first stop is at Thalwil. A freight goes through in the opposite direction whilst on the adjacent track to our left, there is a train of beer wagons.

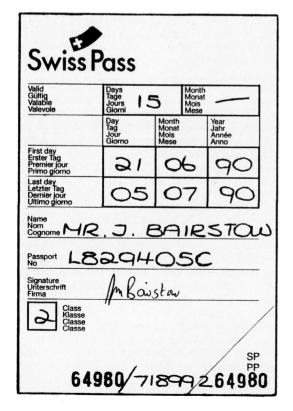

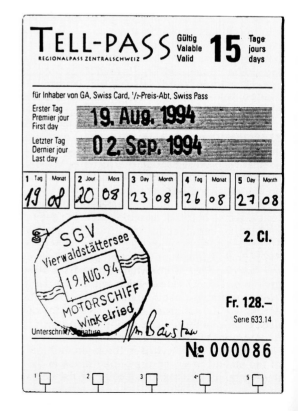

We part company with the lakeshore line, which is actually the main line towards Austria, by a flying junction. As we gain height, we get a better view. We can see the Horgen to Meilen car ferry and a number of passenger ships criss crossing the lake.

Just beyond the station at Horgen Oberdorf, we catch our last glimpse of Lake Zürich then plunge into the 1,985 metre long Zimmerberg Tunnel. After curving through 90 degrees we emerge at Sihlbrugg, the summit of the line which is located in a gorge between two tunnels. We descend at a maximum of 1 in 83 through Albis Tunnel, 3,359 metres in length which takes us from the Canton of Zürich into that of Zug.

As we pass through the station at Baar we notice a little shunting engine standing in front of the goods shed. This is a typical scene at many wayside stations as there is still a volume of traditional freight traffic in Switzerland. Yet the number of big cars parked around the station area confirms that we are in a fully developed western economy. The prosperity of railways here does not stem from any lack of advance in road transport as we may have found on recent trips beyond the old Iron Curtain.

At 12.29, we come to a halt in Zug Station where the main buildings stand in the angle formed by the divergence of the Luzern line from our own route which now continues as a single track the length of Lake Zug.

We enjoy a good view over this lake which is fully circumnavigated by railways. It also has a steamer service which I hope to patronise during this trip having never managed to fit it in before.

The whole scene is now looking quite promising. We have not forgotten our seven days of almost continuous rain last year in Austria. Zürich was a bit cloudy but now the sun is beginning to break through. We are getting closer to the really big mountains. To our right is the Rigi which we hope to ascend by train tomorrow if the weather is clear. Stephen doesn't believe that trains go that high up. We'll show him!

We are now in the Canton of Schwyz, one of the 'Vierwaldstätter', the four Forest Cantons which surround Lake Luzern and which were the first to join the Swiss Confederation in 1271. We pass the head of Lake Zug at Arth am See then continue another two miles to Arth Goldau whose importance as a railway junction far outstrips its size as a town. Here we curve in to join the line from Luzern. To our left is a green and cream electric unit of the Sudostbahn which will have to climb very steeply when it leaves at 13.03 for Einsiedeln. Facing an even steeper climb is the blue and white motor coach and trailer of the Rigi Bahn which starts from its own station at right angles above the Luzern line platforms.

We resume our journey travelling due east in order to get round the small Lake of Lowerz. Straight ahead are the twin peaks of the Gross and Klein Mythen respectively at 1,899 and 1,811 metres above sea level. As we curve southwards towards Steinen, we can see the Sudostbahn high up on a ledge on the hillside to our left. We call at Schwyz Station which is actually some 2 km from this

Schwyz station was at one time called Seewen which was more accurate as the town of Schwyz is some 2km away. The shunting loco on the right is a familiar sight at medium sized Swiss stations.

(Martin Bairstow)

Arrival at Brunnen. Actually No. 11144 on the right is photographed exactly 3 days and 6 hours after our first arrival on the Zürich to Chiasso semi fast. *(Martin Bairstow)*

historic town situated higher up to the east.

Only four minutes now until we alight in Brunnen but there is one railway landmark still worth looking out for. It is just possible to pick out the higher reaches of the Stoos funicular which employs a maximum gradient of 781°/oo (almost 1 in 1¹/₄) to reach the mountain resort of Stoos, 1,290 metres above sea level.

Punctually at 13.04, we arrive at Brunnen Station. Less than 7¹/₂ hours from leaving home, it only remains to walk down the flag bedecked main street towards our hotel, the Brunnerhof (which literally translated could almost mean Fountain Chambers).

A ship pulls into the nearby landing stage. It is the 'Waldstätter' on the 13.15 to Flüelen. Philippa seems to have a soft spot for this vessel possibly because she fears that they are going to withdraw it. We shall renew its acquaintance shortly.

We're soon checked in to the Brunnerhof but we have not come all this way at some expense to sit in a hotel. We have our Swiss Passes and are intending to use them.

One of the attractions in this part of the world is the fleet of lake steamers which includes five superbly maintained paddle vessels. We are at the quayside just in time to photograph the recently refurbished 'Uri' setting off for Luzern at 13.42. Philippa helps Stephen get a shot of it. If this is an example of what 11 days with a Swiss Pass is going to mean, he seems to be adapting to the idea already.

Another paddle steamer has pulled into Treib at the other side of the lake. The two vessels pass in mid channel. We prepare to board the 'Stadt Luzern' for Flüelen.

The first stop is Rütli, the birthplace of the Swiss Confederation. A plaque on board reminds us that General Guisan used this very ship on 25 July 1940 when he travelled to Rütli to plan the defence of Switzerland against Nazi attack. In the event, of course, Swiss neutrality was not violated.

Stephen, like many other passengers both young and old, is more interested in the machinery which drives the paddles. He spends the hour long trip alternately sitting out on deck and retreating to watch the engineer driving what is effectively a steam locomotive (now oil fired) in the bowels of the ship.

The idea had been to catch the 15.33 train back from Flüelen to Brunnen Station in order to collect our fly luggage. The electric multiple unit is already waiting for us when at 15.25 the 'Waldstätter' steams in to Flüelen Pier. Philippa opts to go back on this, her favourite austerity diesel ship created in 1949 out of the remains of an old Thames paddle steamer. No problem – the ticket is equally valid on train or ship.

It only remains to walk back to Brunnen Station to collect our two suitcases. These we must wheel to the hotel but the task is so much easier when hand luggage, coats etc have already been dumped.

So finally we sit down for evening meal in the hotel. Can it only be 24 hours ago that I was waiting, frustrated at Halifax for a train to take me home?

Back in service after a three year refurbishment, the 'Uri' leaves Brunnen for Luzern on 18 August 1994.
(Stephen Bairstow)

Switzerland offers an integrated public transport system. A bus waits outside Flüelen station.
(Martin Bairstow)

The motorship 'Waldstätter' arrives at Flüelen to take us back to Brunnen on 18 August 1994. As Philippa feared, this vessel was withdrawn in 1995. *(Martin Bairstow)*

The handsome exterior of Brunnen Station in August 1987. *(Martin Bairstow)*

Die Schiffahrtsgesellshaft Des Vierwaldstättersees
The Steamers of Lake Luzern

The 'Stadt Luzern' draws into the pier at Beckenried on 28 August 1987.   *(Martin Bairstow)*

It may seem strange to introduce this chapter so early in what is supposed to be a railway book but here the lake steamers are something more than a mere appendix to the railway network. They are at the very centre of it acting as feeders to the various mountain railways, providing transport to lakeside resorts and serving as one of the region's main tourist attractions in their own right. The present fleet of 20 vessels includes five paddle steamers.

Historically, the application of steam power to ships coincided with the development of the railway locomotive. The two forms of transport have always been very closely associated. In Switzerland, the steamship arrived earlier than the railway engine. The latter required tracks which took time to build. The lakes were already there.

The first steamship to ply out of Luzern was, appropriately enough, the paddle steamer 'Stadt Luzern' which entered service on 2 September 1837, almost 22 years before the first railway reached the City.

The 'Stadt Luzern' was built by Escher-Wyss of Zürich, a name which was to have a long association with Swiss paddle steamers. The machinery was supplied by William Fairbairn of Manchester. It was operated by Die Dampfschiffahrtsgesellschaft Des Vierwaldstättersees, a company promoted by the Luzern banker Casimir Friedrich Knörr, to which the concession had been granted by the Canton of Luzern in December 1835.

A second ship, the 'St Gotthard' entered service in 1843 and carried passengers until 1872 when it was converted into a barge to carry materials for the construction of the Gotthard Railway.

The 'Stadt Luzern' operated until 1881 after which the hull was converted into a propeller driven coaling barge. It served in this guise until the last coal burning ship was withdrawn in 1967 after which it was rebuilt again into a bilge water disposal boat.

A rival company appeared in 1847 when Die Post-Dampfschiffahrtsgesellschaft was promoted by Carl Emmanuel Müller of Altdorf. He had previously been responsible for building the road over the Gotthard Pass and was later to build the Axenstrasse between Brunnen and Flüelen. Müller's company gained concessions from the Cantons of Uri and Luzern to operate a service on the lake from 1 November 1847. The first ship, the 'Waldstätter' was joined in April 1848 by the 'Rigi' which is now preserved at the Vehrkehrshaus (Luzern Transport Museum).

Friedrich Knörr agreed to buy out the newcomer in July 1848 but pulled out before the post-Dampfschiffahrtsgesellschaft had chance to ratify the deal. There followed a year of ruinous competition after which the two companies decided that it was better to co-operate. This they did until their amalgamation 20 years later.

The peace was threatened in 1858 when the Schweizerische Centralbahn, which was rapidly laying railway tracks towards Luzern, placed an order with Escher-Wyss for two paddle steamers, the 'Stadt Basel' and 'Stadt Mailand'. The two established steamship operators, Knörr and Müller managed to head off the competition by leasing the two vessels which then operated until the early 1920s.

Competition hotted up again in 1869 with the founding of two new companies. On 18 July Die Dampfschiff-Gesellschaft vom Kussnachtersee started a service on the Kussnacht arm of the lake using a small propeller driven steamship called 'Rütli'.

More serious was the intrusion of Die Dampfschiff-Gesellschaft Luzern which claimed to foresee the need for greater steamship capacity with the increasing number of foreign tourists visiting 'the beautiful banks of the lake' and in the forthcoming opening of the 'Rigibahn'. This organisation ordered two vessels from Sulzer Brothers in Winterthur. The 'Schweiz' and 'Victoria' began life with twin funnels but were lengthened in 1874 and 1876 respectively. The 'Victoria' was destroyed by fire in 1942 but the 'Schweiz' (renamed Schwyz in 1901) continued in service until 1959 when it finally gave way to the present motor ship of the same name. It then served for three years as an overflow restaurant attached to the Hotel Drei Könige in Kussnacht before being scrapped at the age of 93.

To return to 1869, the various shipping concerns decided that their future lay together. This was achieved on 6 July 1870 when they all merged into the Vereinigten Dampfschiffahrts – Gesellschaft des Vierwaldstättersees – the Amalgamated Steamship Company of Lake Luzern.

Hardly had this unity been achieved when in 1871, C. F. Knörr, the pioneer of shipping on Lake Luzern sold most of his shares and used the proceeds to set up a rival Salondampfschiffahrtsge-sellschaft des Vierwaldstättersees which promptly ordered two ships from Escher-Wyss.

This move did not endear Knörr to his fellow shareholders who let their views be known at the 1871 AGM. When Knörr tried to negotiate terms with the VDGV for the leasing of his two ships, the 'Germania' and 'Italia', the latter company was able to knock him down on the price and also to elicit a written undertaking not to engage in any further competition against the established steamship company. This was rather a sad exit from the scene for the pioneer of Lake Luzern shipping. He died in 1882 but the causes of his downfall, the 'Germania' and 'Italia' remained in service until 1949 and 1963

respectively.

With this latest challenge to their monopoly out of the way, the company felt able in 1872 to drop the word Vereinigten (amalgamated) to become Die Dampfschiffahrtsgesellshaft des Vierwaldstättersees. It is the same company today except that in 1960 DGV became SGV when they removed the word "Dampf" (steam) in deference to the growing number of motor ships.

In 1899 the company decided that the growth in tourism necessitated two new ships 'of at least the capacity' of the 'Italia' and 'Germania'. Orders were placed with Escher-Wyss who delivered the 'Uri' in 1901 and with Sulzer who had the 'Unterwalden' ready for service on 15 May 1902. With capacity for 850 passengers, these vessels were the first of a new generation which has survived to the present day – and hopefully for long into the future.

They were followed by the 'Schiller' in 1905, the 'Wilhelm Tell' in 1906, both from Sulzer, and by the 'Gallia' which came from Escher Wyss in 1913.

These were not the largest vessels to have sailed on Lake Luzern. That honour went to the 'Stadt Luzern', the second ship to carry the prestigious name, which had been completed by Escher Wyss in 1887. With a capacity of 1,100 passengers, it was the flagship of the fleet until 1914 when the First World War caused a fall off in tourism. It carried some internees in 1916 but then fell into disuse. It was scrapped in 1925 after a decision had been taken that it would be more cost effective to build a new ship than to persevere with the old one.

The result was the third 'Stadt Luzern' which was built in Germany in 1928. Conveying up to 1,200 passengers, this was the last paddle steamer to enter service in Switzerland. It remains the flagship of the Lake Luzern fleet.

In *Railways in the Austrian Tirol,* I repeated in error the claim that the Achensee steamer 'Stadt Innsbruck' was the first motor ship on a European lake when it entered service in 1912. Not so. The DGV introduced four motor ships between 1910 and 1912. The 'Astra', 'Aero' and 'Mars' were only small vessels carrying between 60 and 80 passengers. Two of them were sold in 1918-20 to the Bern Lötschberg Simplon Railway for use on Lakes Thun and Brienz but the 'Aero' remained in service on Lake Luzern until 1958.

The fourth motor ship which entered service in 1912 was the 'Neptune', rebuilt out of screw driven steamship built by Esher Wyss for service on Lake Zürich. This had capacity for 95 passengers on Lake Luzern where it last ran in 1983.

Two slightly larger diesel ships, the 'Reuss' and 'Rütli' were delivered to Luzern in 1926 and 1929 respectively. They came from the same builders as the 'Stadt Luzern'. With capacity for 135 passengers, they were intended to work between Brunnen and Flüelen and are still in service.

They were joined in 1931 by the 'Mythen' which was built by the DGV itself. This is rather a long slim vessel carrying up to 200 passengers. We found it working daily out of Brunnen in 1994.

The diesel fleet received a further boost in 1949 when the 'Waldstätter' emerged out of the remains of the paddle steamer 'Rhein'. This had begun life in 1905 as the 'Ben Johnson' sailing on the Thames but its owners went into liquidation putting a fleet of 20 vessels onto the market. Learning that their colleagues on Lake Lugano had picked up two bargains, the DGV put in an offer for 'Ben Johnson'. It travelled to Duisburg under its own steam, then was towed to Basel, dismantled and conveyed to Luzern where it was renamed 'Rhein' in honour of the river which had brought it most of the way there. It operated as a paddle steamer until 1939.

The 'Waldstätter' carries 550 passengers. It was joined in 1951 by a new slightly smaller ship the 'Titlis'. Then in 1955 came the 'Rigi' which took the name of the recently withdrawn paddle steamer.

This was the pattern of things to come. In 1959 the paddle steamer 'Schwyz' gave way to a new diesel ship of the same name with capacity for 1,000 passengers. No longer were the diesels just incidental to the steamships. The 'Winkelried', 'Pilatus' and 'Gotthard' followed in 1963-1970, all usurping recently withdrawn paddle steamers.

Delivery of the 'Gotthard' also permitted withdrawal of the paddle steamer 'Wilhelm Tell' which made its last voyage on 4 October 1970. A wave of sympathy was aroused amongst people who had not hitherto bothered too much at the decline of the paddle steamers. The 'Wilhelm Tell' was saved from scrapping and is now permanently moored at the Schweizerhofquai, in Luzern as a restaurant.

Five paddle steamers remained in service but on 1 May 1976, the 'Unterwalden' accompanied a new diesel 'Unterwalden' on its maiden voyage. Afterwards the old vessel was retired.

A support organisation, 'Freunde Der Dampfschiffahrt', formed in the wake of the 'Wilhelm Tell' withdrawal, obtained an assurance from the SGV that the 'Unterwalden' would not be scrapped. They then raised funds to help finance restoration. The steamship re-entered service on 16 May 1985. 11 days earlier, the diesel had celebrated 'Europe day' by changing its name to 'Europa'.

The 'Freunde' went on to help finance major overhauls of the 'Stadt Luzern' and the 'Uri'. They have speculated on whether they should attempt the ultimate challenge, return to service of the 'Wilhelm Tell' but there remains the priority of overhauls for the 'Schiller' and 'Gallia'.

Meanwhile the diesel fleet has not been static. The three years 1990-92 saw delivery of three new medium sized ships, the 'Weggis', 'Flüelen' and 'Brunnen' each with capacity for 400 passengers. These were all additions to the fleet not replacements.

The summer 1994 service operated from 29 May to 25 September. On the main route between Luzern, Brunnen and Flüelen, the service is roughly every hour but it is in no sense a 'taktfahrplan'. Individual sailings have different stopping patterns.

The 'Reuss' at pier No. 2, Brunnen in June 1990. _(Martin Bairstow)_

Some of the intermediate piers are served only two or three times a day. The journey from Luzern to Flüelen takes between 2³/₄ and 3¹/₂ hours each way.

A motor ship (in 1994 usually the Waldstätter) works the first Luzern to Flüelen service at 8.25 then performs various short workings in the Urnersee, between Flüelen and Treib before returning non-stop from Treib to Luzern in 64 minutes. One of the smaller ships is based at Brunnen to provide a few extra crossings to Treib. A larger motor ship is also stabled overnight at Brunnen and one at Flüelen.

There is a departure almost every hour from Luzern to Alpnachstad. The 'Unterwalden' was scheduled to visit Alpnachstad once a day though sometimes it went twice. It is the only paddle steamer which can lower its funnel to get under the bridge which carries the road and railway over a narrow part of the lake between Hergiswil and Stansstad.

The Luzern to Kussnacht service operates three times a day usually with a medium sized ship such as the 'Titlis'. Only very rarely does a paddle steamer venture up the Kussnacht 'branch' of the lake. There is also an hourly local service around Luzern worked by one of the small ships. Rover tickets are not valid 'on capacity grounds'.

Finally there are the night boats which offer a 2 hour cruise out of Luzern 'Mit Musik und Tanz' daily with a motor ship and every Friday with a paddle steamer. Certain other piers also have a night boat once a week in July and August. Only special tickets are valid. In addition there are plenty of private charter sailings.

The timetable in spring and autumn is similar but less intensive. Only one paddle steamer is scheduled to work daily between Luzern and Flüelen.

In winter (from late October until just before Easter), there is no service to Alpnachstad or Kussnacht nor except on Sundays to Flüelen. There are six departures daily from Luzern mostly to Vitznau and Beckenried but the one at 10.30 goes all the way to Rütli. All sailings are non-stop between Luzern and Hertenstein. There is also a smaller ship working out of Brunnen to Treib and once a day to Beckenried where it connects from Luzern.

Travellers from Luzern to Weggis, Vitznau and Gersau are offered the alternative of an SGV bus from the station platform at Kussnacht. This operates all year round and ship tickets are valid on the train and bus.

Swiss Pass and Tell Pass are valid on the lake steamers which, apart from the small vessels, are two class affairs with the upper deck reserved for first class passengers. The medium sized ships have buffet facilities, the larger motor ships and paddle steamers have restaurants.

It goes without saying that most customers are tourists. Some may be just taking a cruise on the lake. Others are using the ship as part of a wider itinerary. The lake steamers are a fully integrated part of 'The Swiss Travel System'.

The 'Pilatus' leaving Brunnen in 1987 before the landing stage was enlarged. *(Martin Bairstow)*

The 'Unterwalden' is now the only paddle steamer which can lower its funnel in order to reach Alpnachstad. Arriving at Luzern in August 1994.   *(Stephen Bairstow)*

The 'Gallia' approaching Treib from Brunnen on 23 August 1994. The Gross and Klein Mythen dominate the skyline.   *(Stephen Bairstow)*

The paddle steamer 'Rigi' ran from 1848 until 1952 covering more than 1¼ million kilometres. Since 1958 it has stood on dry land in the Vehrkehrshaus.
(Martin Bairstow)

The name was transferred to a new motorship launched in 1955. Photographed at Alpnachstad on 20 August 1994, the present 'Rigi' has capacity for 600 passengers.
(Stephen Bairstow)

Dating from 1929, the motorship 'Rütli' has capacity for 140 passengers in second class only. It is seen on 21 June 1990 at its overnight mooring in the Föhnhafen at Brunnen from where it operated a number of crossings to Treib and to Rütli.   *(Martin Bairstow)*

Decorated in celebration of its 25th birthday, the 'Gotthard' is seen between Treib and Gersau on 3 September 1995. *(Martin Bairstow)*

The oldest of the large motor ships, the 'Schwyz' arrives at Beckenried from Luzern on 28 August 1987. Built in 1959, its high bridge and funnel prevent it from going to Alpnachstad. *(Martin Bairstow)*

Dating from 1951, the 'Titlis' has capacity for 400 passengers. It is seen manoeuvring at Luzern. In the background posing as a 'See Restaurant' is the retired paddle steamer 'Wilhelm Tell'. *(Martin Bairstow)*

The 'Winkelried' at pier No. 1 at Luzern in August 1994. The summit of the Rigi is to the right of the Swiss flag.   *(Martin Bairstow)*

The Gotthard Line

11406 'Obwalden', then only a year old, prepares to leave Luzern with a Gotthard express on 15 August 1956. The 120 strong 'Gotthard' class of locos were the first on the SBB to carry names. The tower on the right dominated the façade of the old station. *(John Oxley)*

The train which brought us to Brunnen at the start of our holiday had been bound for Chiasso, the southernmost station in Switzerland. So as we busied ourselves settling into the hotel, our train would have been negotiating the ascent towards the Gotthard Tunnel.

Just over 9¼ miles in length, the tunnel links Göschenen in German speaking Canton Uri with Airolo in Italian speaking Ticino. It provides the only rail link between Ticino and the rest of Switzerland. More than this, it is arguably the most important route between northern and southern Europe which explains why the Governments of both Germany and Italy were willing to assist the Swiss Confederation by contributing to the cost of building it.

Before the railway opened in 1882, the only way across this stretch of the Alps had been by the St Gotthard Pass which reaches a height of nearly 7,000 feet. Since the mid 1830s, the pass had been a road but this is blocked by snow in Winter.

By the late 1860s, ideas for a Trans Alpine railway had been around for 20 years. One proposal was to go from Chur tunnelling into Italy beneath the Splügen Pass – that is some way to the east of the Gotthard route. Another idea was to follow the present Brünig line from Luzern to Meiringen but with a 2¼ mile tunnel under the Brünig Pass, then a 5¾ mile tunnel under the Grimsel Pass to reach

Oberwald in the Rhone Valley, now served by the Furka Oberalp, before tunnelling again, this time for 7¼ miles under the Nufenen Pass, before descending towards Airolo.

The eventual route was determined in 1869 at a conference in Bern at which Italy and various German states were represented. (Germany did not become a single entity until 1871).

Incorporated in November 1871, the Gotthard Bahn was authorised to build 134 miles of railway commencing at Rotkreuz on the existing Luzern to Zürich line and extending as far as Chiasso at the southernmost tip of Switzerland near the border with Italy.

After circumnavigating Lake Luzern, the plan was to use the Reuss Valley to climb up to the 9¼ mile Gotthard Tunnel. Once through the tunnel, the route was to descend through the Leventina Valley eventually skirting Lake Lugano before meeting up with the Italians at Chiasso.

The contractor was Louis Favre from Geneva, who assumed responsibility for planning the route, designing the structures and raising the finance. By the late 1870s, it became clear that private capital alone was not going to be sufficient to complete the project but additional shares were purchased by the Swiss, German and Italian Governments. So it was a multi national part public part private effort which achieved this first major railway conquest of the Alps.

The tunnel opened on 1 January 1882 to be followed five months later by the northern route from Rotkreuz to Göschenen and its southern counterpart from Airolo to Biasca. The line thence to Chiasso being already in use, 1 June 1882 marked the completion of the Gotthard Railway.

Access from both Zürich and Luzern was originally via Rotkreuz, whence the line is carried high above the west shore of Lake Zug to Arth Goldau. It was exactly 15 years later on 1 June 1897 that the shorter route from Luzern opened via Kussnacht to join the existing Gotthard line at Immensee. The same day also witnessed completion of the route along the east side of Lake Zug, from the town of Zug to Arth Goldau giving the more direct route from Zürich – the one which we followed to reach Brunnen from the Airport.

The Gotthard Tunnel was designed for double track but there was a short delay until 1 June 1883 before it was able to be used as such. Doubling over the rest of the route proceeded piecemeal. By 1896, work was complete between Flüelen and Giubiasco, the junction for the Locarno line south of Bellinzona. The most difficult stretches were not dealt with until well into the present century. Immensee to Brunnen was doubled in 1904 but the final stretch, from Brunnen to Sisikon was completed only in 1948, giving continuous double track from Immensee to Chiasso. Rotkreuz to Immensee was doubled in 1963 and work is still continuing on sections between Luzern and Rotkreuz. Luzern to Immensee via Kussnacht and Zug to Arth Goldau still remain single.

Single track was not the only impediment to full exploitation of the Gotthard line. Steam operation must have been a splendid spectacle unless you happened to be the fireman but coal had to be imported and transported considerable distances. Hydro electricity was home produced and, by the second decade of the twentieth century, had been proved capable of offering a more effective service on the severely graded Alpine railways. The entire Gotthard route was electrified between 1920 and 1922 on the standard Swiss voltage of 15,000 ac which is also the norm in Germany and Austria.

By this time, the Gotthard Railway had been nationalised. Established on 1 January 1902, the Swiss Federal Railways were empowered to purchase the hitherto independent railway companies. They took over the Gotthard on 1 May 1909, almost their last acquisition.

The route described – Luzern to Göschenen

Luzern Station has been completely rebuilt since the disastrous fire of 1971. In place of the previous magnificent facade, we now enter through an underground shopping mall. In an attempt to retain some historical perspective, one section of the original portico now stands as a mini Euston Arch or Brandenburg Gate between the steamer terminal and the station.

Luzern is a mixed gauge station with the metre gauge tracks of the Brünig and Engelberg lines accommodated within the main train shed on the eastern most side.

It is, of course, a fully integrated transport interchange with the bus terminal situated adjacent near the upstream end of the steamer quays. Because of the size of the place, the timetable specifies a five minute connectional time between trains (as opposed to the standard two minutes) and ten minutes for changing between train and ship.

As we leave Luzern, we are pointing due south but immediately we turn to the right through almost 180 degrees so that briefly we are heading north. We have a choice of route. If we have intermediate stops then we must adopt the Küssnacht route in which case we will swing to the right at Gütsch. We then cross the fast flowing River Reuss which has come from the Gotthard, has passed through Lake

Underneath the restored archway is this Memorial depicting the façade of Luzern station as it appeared in 1926.
(Martin Bairstow)

Standard and metre gauge at Luzern on 15 August 1956. No. 10426 was a member of a class of 60 introduced in 1925. Just one, No. 10439 survives.
(John Oxley)

Meggen station looking towards Kussnacht.
(Martin Bairstow)

A Luzern bound express passing Kussnacht on 6 September 1988.
(Martin Bairstow)

Luzern and is now on its way to join the Aare, the Rhein and eventually the North Sea.

We enter a long tunnel which takes us under much of the old City of Luzern. Emerging by the lake shore, we can see, opposite, the steamers moored at Luzern Station which we left perhaps eight minutes ago and from which we have travelled at least three miles.

We now pass the Vehrkehrshaus (Swiss Transport Museum) where some of our locomotive's predecessors are standing in one of the display halls parallel to our track. There is no station here. You reach the museum either by steamer or by trolley bus from Luzern.

We follow the lake as far as Seebrugg where we enter a tunnel through which we curve to emerge travelling north east a little way above the Kussnacht arm of Lake Luzern. The first station is Meggen. We may see a ship on its way to or from Kussnacht but even in Summer they only run three times per day on this 'branch'. Towering high on the other side of the lake is the summit of the Rigi which will remain on our right hand side as we circle round it all the way to Arth Goldau.

We are climbing and by Kussnacht are at quite a height above both the town and the lake so if you want to make a train to ship connection here it is best to do it that way round.

If the train stops at Kussnacht, it may connect with a bus on the station platform sporting the livery of the SGV (Steamship Company). This provides a rail bus connection from Luzern to Weggis, Vitznau and Gersau as an alternative to sailing.

There is another abrupt change of direction as we curve in to join the line from Rotkreuz just before Immensee Station which overlooks Lake Zug. We now travel south east with the Rigi to our right and the lake to our left. On the far shore is the line from Zürich which will join us at Arth Goldau. Before this we see down below the head of the lake at Arth am See. There used to be a tramway from there to Arth Goldau but now it is a bus.

At Arth Goldau, the line from Luzern curves in through its own platforms to join the line from Zürich, the actual junction being immediately south of the station. Above the Luzern platforms, and at right angle to them, is the terminus of the Arth Rigi Bahn, the standard gauge rack line whose blue and white trains will take you up to the summit of the Rigi.

The other railway company which shares Arth Goldau is the Sud Ost Bahn whose local trains start from rail level platforms alongside the Zürich side of the station. Expresses come through from Luzern every two hours. They branch off the Gotthard main line immediately south of Arth Goldau to begin a very steep ascent which will take them over the summit of the line at Biberegg and then down towards Lake Zürich at either Wädenswil or Pfäffikon. The main line continues eastward to get round the small lake of Lauerz then swings south at the very historic town of Schwyz which gave its name to the whole country. In fact Schwyz town is over a mile from the station at a higher level. There used to be a tramway from Schwyz station through the town and ending up by the steamer terminal at Brunnen but that journey must now be made on one of the very smart buses of Auto A G Schwyz.

The train passes through Brunnen station then comes alongside the Urnersee, the southern most arm of Lake Luzern. Between Brunnen and Flüelen, you catch the occasional glimpse of the lake. You actually see much more when travelling in the other direction because rather less of the northbound track is in tunnel. The two tracks were built at different times. The original 1882 single line is as close as possible to the lake. It was very difficult to build the second track. When this was finally achieved in 1943 (Sisikon-Flüelen) and 1948 (Brunnen-Sisikon), much of it had to be on a different alignment largely in tunnel.

At Flüelen the train enters the wide Reuss Valley for the easily graded six miles to Erstfeld, a small town tucked away dominated by high mountains, a large railway depot with extensive sidings. The preserved 'Krokodil' No 14270 can sometimes be glimpsed over to the right but is often hidden from view by other rolling stock.

Leaving Erstfeld, the climbing now begins with the next 18 miles at a steady 1 in 38 to 1 in 40 taking us up to Göschenen and the entrance to the Gotthard Tunnel. The line climbs up the east mountain side towards Amsteg beyond which the deep gorge of the Chärstelenbach joins the Reuss Valley. Sandwiched between two tunnels, the Chärstelenbach Viaduct, which was rebuilt in 1971, stands 178 feet above the stream.

The Reuss Valley has now become a steep narrow gorge. Just beyond Gurtnellen, the railway curves into the mountainside entering the Pfaffensprung Tunnel which is a complete spiral. The train emerges 115 feet higher up looking down on the stretch of line over which it has just come.

A mile further on, as we cross the Meienreuss Gorge, look out of the right hand side of train up the gorge and you will see two railway lines at progressively higher levels.

Soon we shall be travelling the first one left to right and then the higher one right to left as we negotiate the Wassen loops. With the aid of several tunnels the railway gains 400 feet. From the top level we can look down and briefly survey some of the works which have got us up here but soon are in the mile long Naxberg Tunnel from which we emerge not far short of Göschenen.

We are not quite at the summit of the line which is reached part way through the 9¼ mile tunnel but this is as far as the engineers could climb in the open. Later on a railway was built to Andermatt but this, the Schöllenen branch of the Furka Oberalp needs rack assistance on its 1 in 5½ climb which takes it over the tunnel mouth and through the series of snow shelters which can be seen heading up towards the sky line.

Push-pull fitted motor coach No. 1464 restarts from Brunnen with a local from Luzern to Göschenen on 13 June 1988. *(Colin Mills)*

Ausflugsbillet
zu Ferienbillet

Gültig **10** Tage

Brunnen
Lugano
mit Bahn-Gotthard
und zurück
ab Flüelen auch mit Schiff

2. Kl. F Fr. 13.90
H 00455 R

11610 'Spreitenbach' heads a northbound freight through Brunnen on 13 June 1988. *(Colin Mills)*

SGV
1/2 Preis
Gültig **1** Tag

Brunnen See
Flüelen
→ 🚢
← 🚢/🚆
←————→

2. Kl.   Fr 6.70
70 03892

Dating from 1931, No. 11801 was the first of three high powered twin units built for the Gotthard Line. Experience showed single locomotives to be more practical. No. 11801 is maintained in working order at Erstfeld and sees occasional use such as this outing on a local freight in Brunnen station on 19 June 1987. *(Colin Mills)*

The Gotthard Tunnel appears to comprise two double track bores but the one on the east (left hand) side merges into the main tunnel after a short distance. It was used by the 'car ferry' trains which started from the now derelict sidings over to our left prior to completion of the motorway tunnel in the 1960s. We end this description of the Gotthard Railway at Göschenen. The train will take less than ten minutes to traverse the tunnel and will then begin its descent through the Leventina Valley employing four spiral tunnels on its way towards Bellinzona, Lugano, Chiasso and maybe beyond into Italy.

Train Services Over The Gotthard

The basic pattern of express service provides that each hour there is a fast and a semi fast. One comes from Luzern and the other from Zürich and both reach Arth Goldau more or less simultaneously. The first to leave Arth Goldau, at 49 minutes past in the 1994/5 timetable, is a 'Euro City' or 'Inter City' first stop Bellinzona then Lugano, Chiasso and on to Milan. Some go a lot further. The 12.49 at Arth Goldau, for example, is the 'Euro City Colosseum', through from Basel to Rome.

The second train leaves Arth Goldau three minutes later for Schwyz, Brunnen, Flüelen, Erstfeld, Göschenen, Airolo, Faido, Biasca, Bellinzona, Lugano and all stations to Chiasso.

On one alternate hour, it is the train from Zürich which is the 'Euro City' and the one from Luzern which is the semi fast. On the other hour it is the opposite way round. In either case, if you find the through service not to your requirement, you either travel an hour earlier or later or you can change at Arth Goldau. This is very much the spirit of the Swiss Taktfahrplan.

Between Luzern and Arth Goldau there are three trains each hour. The one already described leaves at either 14 or 19 past and runs non stop, probably via Rotkreuz. It is preceded at 09 past odd hours only by the 'Voralpen Express' which has an intermediate stop at Kussnacht. This train will be in the green livery of the Sud Ost Bahn or the Bodensee-Toggenburg and is through to St Gallen or possibly Romanshorn on Bodensee (Lake Constance).

Finally there is the local at 27 past from Luzern all stations via Kussnacht to Flüelen. This is often worked by a four coach multiple unit – a modern power car and driving trailer with two refurbished older carriages in the middle.

The local service south of Flüelen was withdrawn with the start of the Summer 1994 timetable. The reason was mainly financial though there was also the question of line capacity. Only the small village stations were affected, those not served by the semi fasts. These places are not, however, forgotten by the SBB. A bus, upon which rail tickets are valid, runs hourly from Göschenen to Erstfeld where it connects into and out of the northbound train before continuing to Flüelen. The buses are more frequent between Erstfeld and Flüelen giving connections into both express and local trains – even into the

lake steamers. The buses serve the 'closed' stations as well as a number of additional request stops.

Not that many of the stations are totally closed. Because the signal box is an integral part of many Swiss stations, they remain open for business and can receive the odd stopping train. On our return from Lugano to Brunnen, we stopped at two of the closed stations on the south side of the Gotthard to pick up passengers. Local events, one of which was an air display, would have caused the bus to be oversubscribed.

Altdorf, the supposed birthplace of the Swiss hero Wilhelm Tell, is left with trains calling only in the early morning and late at night when the Luzern-Flüelen local is extended from and to its stabling point at Erstfeld.

The Gotthard Base Tunnel

The project has been around for the past 35 years – at least. The September 1963 edition of *Modern Railways* carried a feature headed 'The Swiss plan a 28 mile tunnel'.

At that time some 200 trains per day were passing over the Gotthard Line. Efforts had been made to increase capacity: the completion of double track, better signalling and more powerful locomotives. But the SBB calculated that the absolute capacity of the existing route would be reached at 250 trains per day. If traffic grew beyond that, then a radical solution would be required.

Hence the idea of a new 'low level' route between Erstfeld and Biasca which would avoid the mountain section of the existing railway by boring a 45km (28 mile) tunnel from Amsteg to Giornico.

To put the project into perspective, the longest railway tunnel in the World at that time was the 12$\frac{1}{4}$ mile Simplon which pierces the border between Switzerland and Italy south of the Lötschberg. (There is a 17 mile continuous tunnel on the London Underground but that is rather a different proposition). The Channel Tunnel, which opened in 1994, is 31$\frac{1}{4}$ miles long but that will be exceeded by the Gotthard Base Tunnel which is now planned to extend all the way from Erstfeld to Bodio, a distance of 57km (35$\frac{1}{2}$ miles).

The base tunnel plan remained in abeyance for nearly 30 years during which north-south rail capacity was increased by the progressive double tracking of the Bern-Lötschberg-Simplon Railway.

Together, the Gotthard and the Lötschberg/Simplon routes provide the main railway communication between Northern Europe and Italy through Switzerland. The nearest alternative to the east is the Brenner through Austria and to the west the Mont Cénis through France.

Pressure for new capacity comes from the ever increasing volume of freight between Italy and other countries of the European Union most of which must either pass through Switzerland or take a long detour.

Switzerland, which is not a member, refuses to accept demands from the European Union for an

A Flüelen to Luzern emu arrives in Sisikon on 28 August 1994. *(Martin Bairstow)*

11610 'Spreitenbach' is in charge of the following northbound express passing Sisikon on the same day. *(Martin Bairstow)*

increase in the permitted axle load of road lorries from 28 to 40 tonnes. It also imposes a night curfew on lorry movements and charges motorway tolls.

If Switzerland were to adopt a British style transport policy, it would give free access to its road system. It would then pick up the bill for maintaining the roads for international traffic, it would be under constant pressure to build new roads and widen existing ones. This is just unthinkable in Alpine conditions. Apart from the environmental damage, it would result in Swiss residents being crowded off their own roads by international lorries who would make little or no financial contribution.

The solution is 'Die Rollende Strasse' which also features in *Railways in the Austrian Tirol*. The lorries are carried through the Alps by rail but this requires an expansion of capacity.

On 29 May 1996, work finally started on the Gotthard Base Tunnel with the sinking of an access shaft near Sedrun, a town served by the Furka Oberalp. The project has now grown into an entirely new railway all the way from Arth Goldau to Lugano. With a maximum gradient of 1 in 80, the route will not rise higher than 571 metres above sea level compared to the summit of the present line which is at 1,151 metres. The new route will be 40km shorter than the present 171km. It will cater for express passenger trains and freight. The existing route will remain in operation.

Travelling at 200km per hour, passengers will reach Lugano in 40 minutes from Arth Goldau, somewhat faster than the 2¼ hours needed by today's 'Euro Cities'. But the journey will not be as interesting.

Straight after leaving Arth Goldau, the new line will enter the Urmiberg Tunnel. Between Schwyz and Brunnen, it will cross the existing line in the open affording passengers just 27 seconds to admire the Gross and Klein Mythen before plunging into the next tunnel which will take it to Altdorf. It will run alongside the present line to Erstfeld then enter the Gotthard Base Tunnel which will take 20 minutes to get through. Emerging briefly near Biasca, the line will then be underground most of the way to Lugano.

The project is being financed by the Federal Government with the aid of an additional tax on petrol. In addition to all the other legislative hurdles, the project has been approved in a referendum. 2006 is the target date for opening.

10801 entering Flüelen with a southbound passenger train in 1964. Dating from the 1940s, this class of loco disappeared during the 1980s *(Colin Mills)*

'Krokodil' No. 14270 (built 1921) is plinthed at Erstfeld. *(Mike Parsons)*

A northbound tanker train descends through Wassen on 16 June 1988 behind 11668 'Stein–Säckingen'. *(Colin Mills)*

11679 'Cadenazzo' and 11686 'Hochdorf' at Erstfeld Shed on 29 June 1983. Introduced in the mid 1970s, this 90 strong class is an enlarged and uprated successor to the 'Gotthard' class introduced in the 1950s (see page 19). The latter are still running but have generally been superseded on the Gotthard route itself by the newer Bo-Bo-Bo type. *(Mike Parsons)*

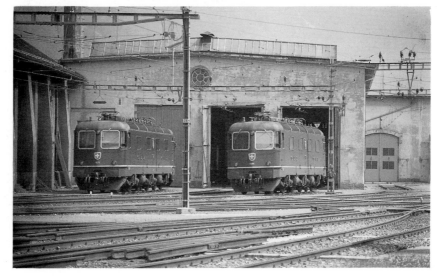

11457 'Romanshorn' emerging from Grumbach Tunnel just north of Flüelen with a southbound express, summer 1964. *(Colin Mills)*

A Flüelen to Luzern local approaching Brunnen on August 1994. The southbound track is in tunnel at this point. *(Martin Bairstow)*

The view from Wassen Church looking north. The freight train has negotiated the Wassen loops and is heading towards Erstfeld, summer 1964.
(Colin Mills)

A six coach 'Trans Europ Express' crossing Mittlere Meienreuss Viaduct on 30 June 1983.
(Mike Parsons)

A few moments later, the same train has now attained the top level. *(Mike Parsons)*

A Krokodil crossing Kellerbach Viaduct with a southbound freight on 4 August 1950.
(John Marshall)

Göschenen station looking north, photographed from a Furka Oberalp train descending from Andermatt. *(Martin Bairstow)*

11656 'Travers' stands in the headshunt at Göschenen having assisted 11618 'Dübendorf' with a heavy freight up from Erstfeld. The assisting engine was marshalled part way through the train in order to lessen the load on the couplings. The train engine is now backing the front half of the train onto the rear part before continuing the journey through the tunnel. *(Colin Mills)*

A northbound express at Göschenen circa 1909. Loco No. 202 was built in 1894 and ran for 30 years.
(John Marshall collection)

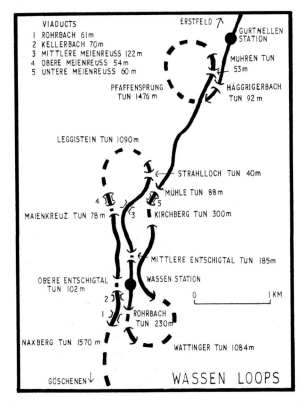

VIADUCTS
1 ROHRBACH 61m
2 KELLERBACH 70m
3 MITTLERE MEIENREUSS 122m
4 OBERE MEIENREUSS 54m
5 UNTERE MEIENREUSS 60m

ERSTFELD
GURTNELLEN STATION
MUHREN TUN 53m
PFAFFENSPRUNG TUN 1476m
HÄGGRIGERBACH TUN 92m

LEGGISTEIN TUN 1090m
STRAHLLOCH TUN 40m
MÜHLE TUN 88m
MAIENKREUZ TUN 78m
KIRCHBERG TUN 300m

MITTLERE ENTSCHIGTAL TUN 185m
OBERE ENTSCHIGTAL TUN 102m
WASSEN STATION
ROHRBACH TUN 230m

NAXBERG TUN 1570m
WATTINGER TUN 1084m

0   1 KM

GÖSCHENEN

WASSEN LOOPS

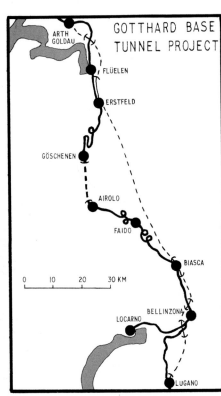

GOTTHARD BASE TUNNEL PROJECT

ARTH GOLDAU
FLÜELEN
ERSTFELD
GÖSCHENEN
AIROLO
FAIDO
BIASCA
BELLINZONA
LOCARNO
LUGANO

0   10   20   30 KM

The Sud Ost Bahn

Arth Goldau stands on the junction where the routes from Luzern and Zürich to the Gotthard converge. The Zürich line points north. Curving to the left are the platforms on the Luzern line. These are crossed on a bridge by the terminus of the Arth Rigi Bahn.

Over to the right of the main Zürich line platforms are a couple of additional tracks – not exactly bay platforms. Arth Goldau still allows passengers to cross the tracks to reach trains which stand at these subsidiary departure points with platforms at no more than rail level.

This is where you will usually find one of the dark green and cream electric multiple units of the Sud Ost Bahn waiting between turns. When departure time comes, this train will set off southwards but, after a very short distance, will branch off the Gotthard Line and begin almost immediately to climb at 1 in 20. Soon Steinen station on the Gotthard line will be seen way below and beyond it Lake Lauerz.

The summit is reached at Biberegg, a request stop 11km from Arth Goldau. Don't incidentally believe the distances in the timetable as this is a line upon which the tariff kilometres are greater than the actual. It is 38km to Rapperswil but the Sud Ost Bahn is allowed to charge as if for 55. The summit level is a plateau of high ground. There is only a slight drop in the next 5km to Altmatt, another request stop. Then begins the equally steep descent which continues most of the way to Pfäffikon.

During the descent, we come to Biberbrugg, junction for the 5km branch to Einsiedeln which curves in at the entrance to the station. If our train is continuing towards Rapperswil, then there will be a connection to the Benedictine Monastic town of Einsiedeln, probably worked by one of the 1940 vintage single railcars in orange livery.

Samstagern is the junction for the line down to Wädenswil, a 1 in 20 descent to join the SBB main line along the shore of Lake Zürich. The main branch of the Sud Ost Bahn continues its own steep descent with excellent views over Lake Zürich, to join the SBB just outside Pfäffikon Station. This is an important junction on the SBB route from Zürich to Chur and to Austria.

The remaining stretch of the Sud Ost Bahn to Rapperswil runs over the Seedamm, the road and rail causeway which was built in 1878 across the shallow waters of Lake Zürich virtually dividing it in two. There are bridges so that ships can still pass underneath.

The Sud Ost Bahn was created on 1 January 1890 by the amalgamation of the Wädenswil-Einsiedeln and Zürichsee-Gotthard Railways. The former was opened in 1877 and the latter between Rapperswil and Pfäffikon only on 27 August 1878. It was not until after the amalgamation that the through route was created with the opening in 1891 of the Pfäffikon-Samstagern and Biberbrugg-Arth Goldau sections.

Always single track, the entire network was electrified, on the standard SBB system on 15 May 1939.

A fairly extensive local service is offered with four trains an hour on the Einsiedeln branch and virtually a half hourly frequency from Biberbrugg to Wädenswil. There is a local train every hour from Arth Goldau going alternately to Einsiedeln or to Rapperswil and beyond.

The prestige passenger service over the Sud Ost Bahn is the two hourly 'Voralpen Express' from Luzern to St Gallen or Romanshorn. This is a loco hauled train which brings together stock of the three participating railways: the SBB, the Sud Ost Bahn and the Bodensee Toggenburg. These trains stop intermediately on the Sud Ost Bahn only at Biberbrugg, Wollerau and Pfäffikon.

SOB No. 41 at Arth Goldau in 1982. Similar to the 273 strong SBB Class (11101-11397), this loco was delivered new to the SOB in 1967. It has since been joined by three others bought second hand from the SBB.
(Mike Parsons)

The gradient is apparent as one of the ex SBB locos sweeps into Samstagern from Arth Goldau on 7 September 1988. *(Martin Bairstow)*

A Romanshorn to Luzern 'Voralpen Express' pauses at Arth Goldau. The latest type of Sud Ost Bahn air conditioned coach is drawn by SBB No. 10102, one of four experimental locos built in 1982, which may have since been sold to the SOB. *(Martin Bairstow)*

The Einsiedeln train awaits its 'main line' connection at Biberbrugg on 1 September 1987. *(Martin Bairstow)*

Two of the 1940 built single railcars wait on the north side of the SBB Main line in Pfäffikon station on 1 September 1987. No. 13 'Richterswil' and No. 11 'Burghalden'. *(Martin Bairstow)*

The Seetal Bahn

Birrwil looking north. The high visibility paint on the driving trailer and the roadside location confirm
that we are on the Seetalbahn. *(Martin Bairstow)*

What identifies the Lenzburg train as it stands in Luzern Station is the high visibility marking on the front ends of the locomotive and driving trailer. This is an attempt to limit the number of accidents caused by motorists who venture too close to the trains as they negotiate the 400 or so level crossings along what is little more than a roadside tramway through the Seetal or Lake Valley.

For the first 5 km out of Luzern, the Lenzburg train takes the double track main line towards Olten. But restarting from the first station at Emmenbrücke, it just rolls forward into a headshunt where it comes again to a stand. The driver climbs down from the locomotive and makes his way to the cab at the rear of the end carriage. And then we are off the other way for the rest of the journey which will lead eventually to a terminal platform in the station forecourt at Lenzburg, 37 km to the west of Zürich on the main line from there to Olten and Basel.

The Seetalbahn is steeply graded with climbs of up to 36°/oo (= 1 in 28). Opened in 1883, it was built on the cheap. Earlier schemes had failed for lack of finance. The line, as built, was the brainchild of Theodor Lutz (1841-1900), a Zürich engineer who favoured construction along the existing road through the valley. This would not only reduce cost but would enable the line to penetrate the centres of the villages. Lutz travelled first to Paris and then to London in a bid to gain financial backing for his idea which he hoped would find wider application. So this slightly unconventional Swiss railway was built with British capital.

There is nothing unique about a railway running along the roadside. In steam days speed would have been slow but, as Lutz pointed out, there was the compensation of reaching the population. Many such lines disappeared once the internal combustion engine had proved its reliability. Sometimes the tracks were coveted for road widening. In Switzerland, a number of narrow gauge lines still make use of roadside rights of way. With electric traction they can offer an effective service. What makes the Seetalbahn different is that it now forms part of the main SBB network.

For the first 20 years after 1883, the Seetalbahn operated 0-6-0 tank engines hauling four wheel carriages. Journey time was 2¼ hours for the 41 km between Emmenbrücke and Lenzburg. They started running carriages through to Luzern in 1894, attached to trains of the Swiss Central Railway at Emmenbrücke.

In 1902 the Seetalbahn took delivery of some more powerful 2-6-0 tanks. The following year they acquired three bogie, that is eight wheel, buffet cars, the first to operate in Switzerland.

The next major development was electrification, inaugurated in 1910, at 5,500 volts ac. Eight passenger motor coaches were employed bringing the Emmenbrücke – Lenzburg time down to 1¾ hours.

During the First World War, the Seetalbahn enjoyed a measure of prosperity as, unlike its neighbours, it could operate free from dependence on imported coal. Then, rather surprisingly, the line was nationalised on 1 January 1922, becoming a part of the SBB. Formed in 1902, the SBB had virtually reached its present size when it took over the Gotthard Bahn in 1909. The Seetal line was one of the very few additions after that date.

The SBB invested in the infrastructure of the Seetal line. With heavier trains and a growing volume of road traffic, it became desirable to segregate the two. Gradually the railway was relaid on conventional railway track separate but not fenced off from the road surface.

The main line from Olten to Luzern was electrified in 1924 on the standard SBB system at 15,000 volts ac. Through trains from the Seetal were still hauled by steam from Emmenbrücke into Luzern.

Steam returned in full strength to the Seetal line for the 1930 summer timetable whilst conversion work took place on the electrification system. 15,000 volt working commenced on 1 October that year.

Today the Seetal line enjoys a basic hourly service with a journey time of 1 hour 20 minutes from Luzern to Lenzburg.

Beinwil – Beromünster

The branch from Beinwil to Menziken opened on 23 January 1887. In 1904, it was joined in Menziken Station by the narrow gauge Wynental und Suhrentalbahn from Aarau. The question then arose of how to build an extension southwards: narrow gauge WSB or standard gauge Seetalbahn. The metre gauge line would have had the facility to transport standard gauge wagons on 'rollbocke' so it would have offered competition to the Seetalbahn had it been projected right through to Emmenbrücke.

So the Seetalbahn applied successfully to extend its own branch from Menziken as far as Beromünster. This opened on 1 October 1906 and was electrified with the rest of the Seetalbahn in 1910. The climb up to Beromünster included a stretch at 37°/oo (1 in 27) the steepest gradient on the SBB (apart from the rack sections of the Brünig Line).

With the May 1992 timetable change, the passenger service was withdrawn from the 8 km branch between Beinwil and Beromünster. The reason was financial. In fact the argument will be very familiar to British readers who were around during the 1960s. According to the SBB, costs were running at 12 times the revenue. Against this, it was argued in *Schweizer Eisenbahn Review* (May 1992) that up to half the costs could be avoided if the SBB would adopt working practices already familiar on many of the Swiss private railways.

Be that as it may, the trains were withdrawn but, unlike British practice of 30 years ago, the line was not just forgotten. The trains were replaced by a bus service subcontracted to the Post Office. This is subsidised by the Federal Government at a sum quoted as about one fifth the cost of continuing with the railway. Rail tickets are valid and through bookings can still be made. The bus driver is in radio contact with the SBB. The bus is slower than the train used to be but, thanks to an extra subsidy from the Canton of Luzern, it serves the village of Schwarzenbach, between Borumünster and Menziken which previously had no public transport.

Manual block in operation at Eschenbach.

(Martin Bairstow)

Beinwil 22 August 1994. A southbound freight, just visible beyond the Beromünster bus, is about to cross the 13.01 Luzern to Lenzburg. *(Martin Bairstow)*

The Hallwilersee Schiffahrt

The scale of shipping activity on Hallwilersee is constrained by its small size. Comprising only 10 sq. km. of water, the lake has sometimes been nicknamed Halblitersee (½ litre sea). Nevertheless, in 1888, a service was started to give the villages on the right bank a connection into the new railway.

The Seetalbahn took control of the operation in 1890, employing a propeller steamer 'Hallwyl', a product of Escher – Wyss with capacity for 70 people. Unfortunately, this modest craft proved far too large for the traffic on offer so in 1891 the service was restricted to Summer Sundays only.

A smaller ship 'Seetal' was launched in March 1893. Only 11.5 metres long and 2.6 metres wide, this tiny propeller steamer could carry up to 30 passengers with a choice of first and second class! Results continued to disappoint. The Railway Company pulled out in 1896 leaving operation in the hands of the Halwilersee Steamship Company.

The service struggled on. The two steamships were replaced by slightly larger motor ships in 1911 and 1918. In more recent times the service has grown with the tourist industry.

Today the ships run from April to October but on Sundays only in the first and last few weeks of the season. The basic service runs anti clockwise from Meisterschwanden to Birrwil, Beinwil and back. On Summer Sundays there is a much more comprehensive service reaching more destinations. Most sailings have buffet facilities, a successor to the pioneer service on the Seetalbahn which expired in the 1940s.

The easiest train to ship interchange is at Mosen but that is only served on Sundays. Beinwil and Birrwil are respectively 750 and 500 metres distance but at both it is a steep climb up from the lake to the station. Meisterschwanden – Delphin landing stage is 1,500 metres from Fahrwangen – Meisterschwanden Station on the branch from Wohlen.

The 'Fortuna' pulling away from Birrwil on 22 August 1994. *(Martin Bairstow)*

38

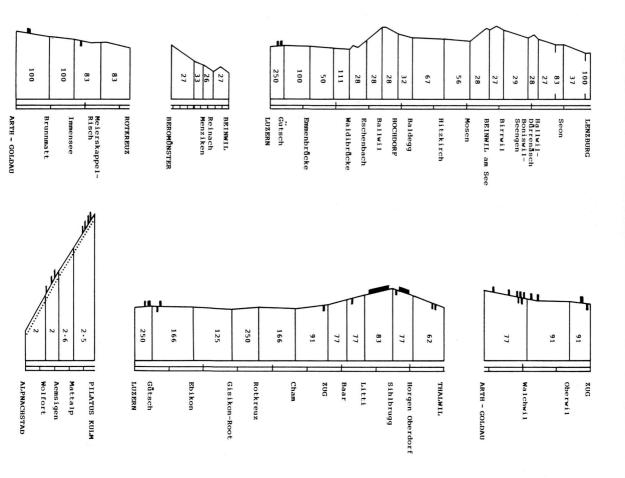

The gradient profiles are expressed in the British 'one in so many' rather than the Continental 'so many per thousand'. The gradients are the maximum between the points stated. British style profiles showing exact gradients would be totally impractical.

Top left: Rigi Kulm, 19 August 1994. Beginning the descent towards Vitznau is railcar No. 3 dating from electrification of the line in 1937.　　　　　　　　　　　　　　　　　*(Martin Bairstow)*

Bottom left: The steepest rack railway in the world climbs to the summit of Pilatus, viewed on a reasonably clear 30 August 1987.　　　　　　　　　　　　　　　　　*(Martin Bairstow)*

Top right: The upper terminus of the Treib Seelisberg Bahn, 21 June 1990.　　　　　　*(Martin Bairstow)*

Bottom right: Driving trailer No. 26 brings up the rear of the 9.45 Engelberg to Luzern which has just restarted from Stans on 26 August 1994.　　　　　　　　　　　　　　*(Martin Bairstow)*

The Brünig Line

The 17.17 departure from Meiringen to Luzern begins the rack ascent on 17 September 1992. 101-965 'Lungern' is piloted by one of the 1941 built locos.
(Colin Mills)

'What connects the paddle steamer 'Uri' with the paddle steamer 'Lötschberg?' So asked an advertisement for the Brünig Line a few years ago. The Brünig Line links two of the most popular tourist centres in Switzerland: Lake Luzern and the Bernese Oberland. 74km in length, it is the only narrow gauge and the only rack line belonging to the SBB.

When first opened on 1 June 1888, the line really did connect the predecessors of the 'Uri' and the 'Lötschberg', the steamers of Lake Luzern and Lake Brienz because the trains only ran between Alpnachstad and Brienz. Access to Luzern and to Interlaken was by ship. It took only until the following year to complete the link into Luzern but it was not until 1916 that trains began to negotiate the heavily engineered lakeside route between Brienz and Interlaken.

At 1,008 metres above sea level, the Brünig Pass offers the only possible route for a railway. To the west the Brienzer Rothorn stands at 2,350 metres. To the east the Giebel 2,036 metres. In the 1860s, there was a proposal to build the Trans Alpine railway this way. It would have employed a 3.5km tunnel under the Pass. It was eventually built further east as the Gotthard Line.

There was a proposal in the 1870s for a standard gauge line between Alpnachstad and Brienz with a tunnel under the Brünig Pass. A concession was

obtained and a subsidy was agreed by the Canton of Bern after a referendum. But the scheme fell victim to a downturn in the economic cycle and the promoters looked for a cheaper alternative, a line more 'local and touristic in character'.

The gauge was narrowed to metre, gradients made steeper, curves sharper and rack working introduced so that the line could go over rather than in tunnel under the Brünig Pass. The Jura-Bern-Luzern Railway was asked to build and operate the line. This is how the line comes to be part of the SBB. It was owned by one of the main line companies at the time of nationalisation. The Jura-Bern-Luzern became part of the Jura-Simplon in 1890 and was taken into the SBB on 1 May 1903.

Single track throughout, the line starts on the eastern side of Luzern station sharing platforms with trains of the Luzern-Stans-Engelberg which travel over the same track for the first 8km to Hergiswil.

As far as Horw, the route is industrial and suburban but at Hergiswil Matt it comes alongside Lake Luzern. The southern tip of the lake is reached at Alpnachstad, lower terminus of the Pilatus Bahn.

The line climbs modestly through the valley of the Sarn skirting the full length of Sarnersee until Giswil is reached. In steam days there would have been a change of loco for the rack section. Until fairly recently we might have been piloted by one of

A 'mixed' descending the rack into Giswil in 1964. There is still freight on the adhesion sections in standard gauge wagons but no narrow gauge freight and none over the mountain. *(Colin Mills)*

the mountain locos 'Giswil' or 'Meiringen'. But since 1990, almost all express trains are whisked over the pass by one of the eight class 101 BO-BOs, all named after places along the route. There are three rack sections on the climb from Giswil to the summit which is reached in Brünig-Hasliberg Station. Maximum gradient is 1 in 10 increasing to 1 in 9 on the last leg up from Käppell. The train slows down as it approaches the start of each rack section. There is a sign on the trackside marked 'A' (Anfang = beginning). On the other side it reads 'E' (Ende). There is a bang under the carriage as the rack wheels engage. Then the train accelerates a little with a slight grinding sensation.

Straight out of Brünig-Hasliberg the descent begins at 1 in 8. The line is perched on a ledge above the Aare Valley. Slowly it drops towards the valley floor where it comes alongside the track from Interlaken just before the entrance to Meiringen Station. This is a dead end and the train must reverse. Usually a fresh engine appears at the other end for the remaining 29km to Interlaken Ost.

There is one other rail route out of Meiringen, the tiny Innertkirchen Bahn which begins from a little halt on the south east side of the main station. It cannot run onto Brünig line tracks because of the different voltage.

Continuing to Interlaken, the line follows the wide Aare Valley. Approaching Brienz it comes alongside the lake. Outside Brienz Station is the Rothorn Bahn, one of the very few remaining non electrified railways in Switzerland. In Summer steam and diesel locos propel trains up an almost steady 1 in 4 to the summit.

The remaining 16km of the Brünig Line are along the lake side with a number of tunnels and cuttings blocking the view intermittently until the railway crosses the River Aare close to its exfluence from the Lake. It then descends into Interlaken Ost for interchange with the standard gauge Bern Lötschberg Simplon and metre gauge Berner Oberland Railways.

In steam days, the through journey took up to 3½ hours. The Railway started off with a fleet of 0-6-0 locos for the non rack sections and eight, later increased to 13, 0-4-0s for working between Giswil and Meiringen. In common with most rack steam locomotives, these had sloping boilers to compensate for the prevailing gradient. If running beyond Brünig – Hasliberg, they had to turn on the turntable there. They pulled trains uphill (on steeper rack lines, the engine normally pushes).

The fleet was totally replaced around 1910 with 12 larger 2-6-0 tanks non rack fitted and 18 0-6-0 tanks capable of working both rack and non rack. Most of the steam locos were withdrawn upon

43

Hergiswil station with an express for Interlaken being passed by a push-pull from Giswil in August 1994. Brünig line tunnel, Lopper 1, to the right. LSE, Lopper 2, to the left. *(Martin Bairstow)*

908 in charge of three standard gauge tankers at Giswil in June 1986. The banners proclaiming 'Kinder Reisen Gratis Mit' herald the introduction of free travel for accompanied children from 1 July that year.
(Martin Bairstow)

electrification but a few survived into the 1960s on shunting and emergency duties.

A new design of rack steam loco was under discussion in 1926 when it seemed that electrification was a long way off. This was delayed in part by indecision over whether to regauge the line to standard or to bypass the rack sections. In the event, the infrastructure remained unchanged and the line was electrified on the standard SBB system at 15,000 volts ac in 1940-42.

16 'gepäcktriebwagen' (locomotives with luggage accommodation) reduced the journey time for express trains to under two hours. They were joined in 1954 by two 'mountain' locos purpose built for passenger work on the rack section, which helped to reduce the incidence of double or even triple heading.

The first of the new generation of motive power arrived in 1985 although the prototypes were sold on to the Furka Oberalp Railway when the eight production models arrived in 1989/90.

The present day timetable has an express leaving Luzern at 24 minutes past every hour calling at Hergiswil, Sarnen and then all stations to Meiringen. One alternate hour it continues fast to Interlaken Ost stopping only at Brienz. On the other it goes forward all stations. Through journey time is 1 hour 52 or 1 hour 59 minutes.

The fast train is preceded out of Luzern at 9 minutes past by a local to Giswil. This is worked by one of the 'gepäcktriebwagen' from 1941, now fitted for push-pull operation, since relegation from express duties. A push-pull set also works one or two extra trips between Meiringen and Interlaken Ost.

Standard gauge freight vehicles can be accommodated on 'rollbocke' but not over the mountain section.

0-4-0T No. 354 on the Husenbach Bridge, a short way up the climb out of Meiringen, about 1889.
(Martin Bairstow

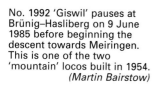

No. 1992 'Giswil' pauses at Brünig–Hasliberg on 9 June 1985 before beginning the descent towards Meiringen. This is one of the two 'mountain' locos built in 1954.
(Martin Bairstow)

The 9.20 Interlaken Ost to Luzern negotiates the curves between Lungern and Kaiserstuhl on 15 August 1956. *(John Oxley)*

The same train passes loco No. 912 on the 11.06 from Luzern at Alpnachstad. *(John Oxley)*

101-961 'Horw' leaves the rack as it nears Meiringen with a Luzern to Interlaken express on 16 September 1992. *(Colin Mills)*

Interlaken Ost, terminus of the Brünig Line. *(Martin Bairstow)*

Luzern – Stans – Engelberg

LSE No. 5 at Engelberg on 28 August 1987.   *(Martin Bairstow)*

The December 1964 issue of *Modern Railways* makes no less depressing reading now than the day it was published. Within the first two pages, there is the Minister of Transport's approval for '40 or so' closures, there is Harold Wilson's broken pledge over Whitby and a doubling of the charge for using the toilets at certain London stations. It was only the last mentioned item which failed to gain editorial approval.

But tucked away towards the end of the journal is a paragraph headed 'Switzerland, the Lucerne-Engelberg Link'. At least there was one corner of the World where transport policy was following a more enlightened course.

The event reported was the opening on 19 December 1964 of the short link between Hergiswil and Stansstad. Just over a mile and a half in length, mostly in tunnel or on a viaduct, this long awaited development had the effect of ending the isolation of the metre gauge Stansstad-Engelberg Bahn.

Previously this 14 mile line had operated from the steamer terminal at Stansstad to the mountain resort of Engelberg. Travellers from Luzern had to start out by ship changing at Stansstad, a total journey of two hours. The rail portion was not fast taking one hour for the 14 miles. From Obermatt to Ghärst, the electric multiple unit had to be propelled up the 1 in 4 rack

section by a small 0-4-0 locomotive.

The idea of linking the Engelberg line to the Brünig at Hergiswil had been around for some time. The possibility is mentioned in the 1953 edition of *Switzerland's Amazing Railways*. Eventually the project went ahead in conjunction with the new concrete road viaduct which replaced the previous opening span across the narrow stretch of water which almost separates Alpnachersee from the rest of Lake Luzern.

The Engelberg Railway was relaid for higher speeds, converted from three phase to the standard SBB electrification at 15,000 volts ac and re-equipped with five three car train sets, rack fitted so that they could drive themselves up and down the 1 in 4. Three more identical units were added between 1970 and 1980.

The train service was extended through from Luzern to Engelberg. The Stansstad steamer was reduced to Summer only and the Hergiswil to Beckenried postbus withdrawn between Hergiswil and Stansstad but retimed to connect with the new train service. The Railway changed its name to the Luzern-Stans-Engelberg.

Stans is the capital of the half Canton of Nidwalden, the historic Canton of Unterwalden being divided in two for administrative purposes. The railway came to Stans in August 1893 with the opening of both the Stanserhornbahn and the Strassenbahn Stansstad-Stans. The former was a funicular in three sections, featured later in the book. The latter was one of the earliest electric tramways in Switzerland, a metre gauge line running from the landing stage at Stansstad to the Post Platz at Stans, just beyond the lower terminus of the Stanserhornbahn.

The tramway was eclipsed somewhat in October 1898 with the opening of the Stansstad-Engelberg Railway which ran closely parallel. The two lines crossed just outside Stans, a short dead section being required in the overhead to separate the 500 volts dc on the tramway from the 750 volts three phase of the Engelberg line. The tramway could not compete. It was taken over by the Stansstad-Engelberg Company and then shut down on 30 September 1903.

The Railway continued with its original rolling stock until the changes in 1964. Since then it has relied on the eight three car train sets which appear in red livery. They were refurbished internally during the 1980s, upholstered seats replacing the more austere 1960s style. In 1991, the LSE bought two ex Brünig locos to create two push-pull sets for working over the non rack sections.

The LSE offers a basic hourly service taking just under an hour from Luzern to Engelberg. There are one or two extras between Luzern and Stans. On Sundays in both mid summer and mid winter, there is the 'Titlis Express' at 8.01 from Luzern which completes the journey non-stop in 43 minutes, clearly aimed at those heading by cable car to Trubsee, Jochpass and the Kleintitlis.

During 1995 Federal and Cantonal funds were voted for the construction of a new alignment to bypass the 1 in 4 climb up to Engelberg. Still rack worked, the new line will climb at no more than 1 in 8 allowing longer trains to run through to Engelberg including rolling stock off the Brünig line which is not allowed on the present LSE rack section.

The Lopperberg towers above the narrow stretch of water which separates Alpnachersee from the rest of Lake Luzern. In the middle foreground is Stansstad station and motive power depot. The railway crosses the water on the near side of the road-rail bridge then enters the 1,743 metre Lopper 2 Tunnel.

(Martin Bairstow)

Standard gauge freight wagons at Stans on 28 August 1987. A passenger train arrives from Luzern.

(Martin Bairstow)

Gültig **2** Tage
Klassenwechsel

Engelberg
Luzern

via Hergiswil 🚋

1. Kl.   Fr 3.20

Engelberg - Luzern
via Hergiswil 🚋
Klw. ■ Fr 3.20

00127

Stansstad motive power depot on 26 August 1994. The main line climbs up on the left to come alongside the adjacent road for the lake crossing.

(Martin Bairstow)

T1   DGV
Gültig **10** Tage

Luzern See
Engelberg
und zurück

via Stansstad

2. Kl.   Fr 9.—

T1   Luzern - Engelberg   DGV
via Stansstad
H   ■ Fr 9.—   **R**

00436

LSE trains share the Brünig line between Hergiswil and Luzern but do not normally stop at Hergiswil Matt which relies on the hourly Giswil push-pull, seen here on 25 August 1994.

(Martin Bairstow)

LSE No. 2 prepares to stop by request at Grünenwald on 28 August 1987.　　　　*(Martin Bairstow)*

The same train descends into Obermatt where a train from Luzern is waiting to begin its climb up the 1 in 4 rack section.　　　　*(Martin Bairstow)*

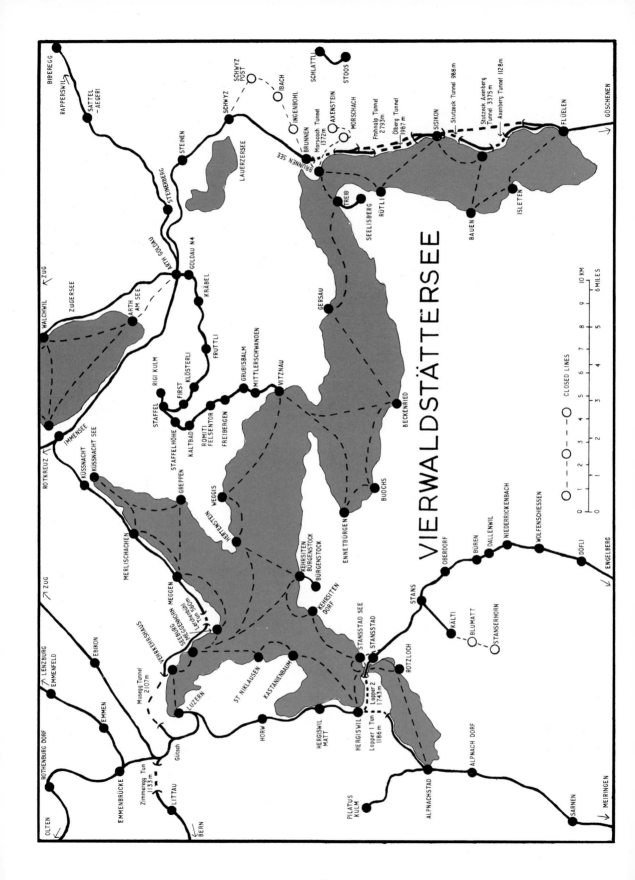

Rigi Bahnen

Rigi Kulm on 19 August 1994 with a train for Arth Goldau. Milk traffic on the platform. *(Martin Bairstow)*

The oldest mountain rack railway in the world is that which ascends Mount Washington in New Hampshire USA. Opened in 1869, it predated the first Swiss line by just two years.

Niklaus Riggenbach, locomotive engineer of the Swiss Central Railway had patented a rack system in 1863 but had not been able to apply it anywhere. When he heard about the Mount Washington line, Riggenbach visited the USA to see it in operation.

On return to Switzerland, he and his associates lost little time in obtaining a concession from the Canton of Luzern to build a line from Vitznau, on Lake Luzern, to Staffelhöhe, 2 km in distance and 200 metres in height short of the summit of the Rigi.

The line opened on 23 May 1871. It was standard gauge, steam operated with a maximum gradient of 1 in 4. Riggenbach's system involved laying a kind of steel ladder in the centre of the track into which cogwheels on the locomotive could engage. The rungs of this ladder are tapered. Riggenbach considered this feature an improvement on the round ones at Mount Washington.

Plans to extend the line to the summit itself were frustrated briefly by the Canton of Schwyz declining to extend the concession onto its territory. They preferred to give their support to a rival concern which planned a line from Arth Goldau to the top of the Rigi.

From 1872, the power to grant railway concessions was transferred to the Federal Government but the Canton of Schwyz had already given one to the Arth Rigi Bahn.

On 27 June 1873, the link was opened between Staffelhöhe and Rigi Kulm (summit). Built by the Arth Rigi Bahn, operation was entrusted to the original Rigi Bahn.

4 June 1875 saw the opening of the Arth Rigi Bahn itself, all the way from the lakeside at Arth am See via Arth Goldau, where the rack section began to Rigi Kulm. A second parallel track was provided between Staffel and Rigi Kulm alongside that used by the trains from Vitznau.

Meanwhile a branch had opened from Kaltbad, on the line from Vitznau, along the crest of the ridge to Scheidegg. 7 km in length, this was closed by the railway company on 21 September 1931 but then operated summer only from 1933 until 1942 by local hoteliers.

The first Rigi Bahn locomotives were strange looking 2-2-0 tanks with vertical boilers. No 8 is preserved at the Vehrkehrshaus.

Later they changed to the more familiar 0-4-2 tanks with boilers leaning forward to compensate at least partially for the prevailing gradient. Nos 16 and 17, dating from 1923 and 1925, are retained at Vitznau for occasional use.

By the time these were built, the Arth Rigi line had been electrified for some time. The tramway between Arth am See and Arth Goldau was converted from steam to electric on 1 January 1906. The mountain section followed on 20 May 1907.

It was not until 3 October 1937 that electric traction began between Vitznau and Rigi Kulm. The Arth am See to Arth Goldau line closed on 31 August 1959.

Today the two Rigi lines are operated under one management. Both function all year round. The service from Arth Goldau is hourly, though with some variations. That from Vitznau is more erratic as many departures are timed to give tight connections with the lake steamers.

The ascent from Vitznau is the more dramatic. The best view is on the left hand side of the carriage.

As far as Staffelhöhe, the view is west towards Pilatus and Luzern. Then the Kussnacht arm of the lake comes into view. From the summit there is plenty to see in all directions, at least on a clear day.

The route from Arth Goldau is not quite as steep. The train climbs up the precipitous Kräbelwand before turning into the valley of the Sagenbach which divides the Rigi in two. By the time First Station is reached, the summit is in sight but still a long way up. The Vitznau line is joined in Staffel Station from where the two routes run in parallel to the summit at Rigi Kulm.

Fare are high. The Swiss Pass and Swiss Card give a 25% reduction which was also available on production of the guest card issued at the hotel. The Tell Pass is valid for unlimited travel.

Vitznau station seen from the lake in 1987.
(Martin Bairstow)

```
        SGV
      ½ Preis
   Gültig 1 Monat
   Rundfahrt 105
      Brunnen
      Vitznau
      Rigi Kulm
     Arth-Goldau
      Brunnen
   oder umgekehrt
  2. Kl.    Fr 24.20
  70 00171
```

No. 22 pauses at Kaltbad on 23 August 1994.
(Martin Bairstow)

Loco No. 18, built 1938, with a works train in Rigi Staffel station in August 1994.
(Martin Bairstow)

Driving trailer No. 21 in the Rigi Bahn terminus above the Luzern–Gotthard platforms at Arth Goldau on 31 August 1987.   *(Martin Bairstow)*

Latest stock on the Arth Rigi Bahn, No. 15 at the summit in August 1994.
(Stephen Bairstow)

Rigi Staffel is where the two routes converge for the final assault on the summit. No. 11 has come up from Arth Goldau. The Vitznau platform is on the left. *(Martin Bairstow)*

Vitznau Rigi Bahn No. 4, built 1953, propels a vintage trailer up the double track section just below Kaltbad on 23 August 1994. *(Philippa Simpson)*

Pilatus – The Steepest Rack Railway in the World

At 480°/oo (almost 1 in 2), the Pilatus Bahn is the steepest rack railway in the world. Above the trees to the left of the train there is an avalanche shelter. Hopefully, one can then make out the alignment climbing very steeply to the left on a ledge on the rock face. *(Martin Bairstow)*

Dominating the skyline to the south of Luzern is the Pilatus which at 2,129 metres above sea level is not only higher than the Rigi but a great deal steeper and much wilder. It would not have been possible to ascend Pilatus using the Riggenbach or any similar rack system which is effectively limited to a maximum gradient of 1 in 4.

When Colonel Edouard Locher planned a line from Alpanachstad to the summit of Pilatus, he had to invent his own unique rack system in order to conquer a height difference of 1,633 metres in only 4.8 km. That gives an average gradient steeper than 1 in 3 with a maximum of 48% – almost 1 in 2.

The Locher system has a rack rail with two parallel sets of horizontal teeth which are engaged by double horizontal pinion wheels underneath each carriage. Besides providing traction and braking, the pinion wheels hold the carriage on the track making it unnecessary for the running wheels to have any flanges.

The line opened on 4 June 1889. It is laid to 80cm gauge and for the first 48 years was steam operated. Journey time was 1 hour 25 minutes. This was shortened to 30 minutes up, 40 minutes down when electrification was inaugurated on 15 May 1937.

The eight motor coaches built in 1937 are still in operation. Two more were added in the 1960s to give a maximum capacity of five coaches in each up and downhill timetable path. They cannot run in multiple so each departure involves between one and five independent coaches according to the volume of traffic.

The line operates from the middle of May to the end of November, the precise dates depending on the weather. The service reaches a peak of 16 departures each way during July and August.

Fares are very high at 53 francs return in 1994. You could travel 110 km return for that on the SBB, 23 times the distance. Holders of the Swiss Pass and Swiss Card get a 25% reduction. The line is included on the Tell Pass.

An alternative route is by trolley bus from Luzern to Kriens then by gondelbahn (cabin lift) to Fräkmüntegg and cable car to the summit. Circular tour tickets are advertised from Luzern to Pilatus out by train or steamer via Alpnachstad and back via Kriens or vice versa.

The perennial problem is that on a really good day, it can be so busy that some passengers are unable to board the service of their choice and have to queue for the next one. Then on a poor day you may see nothing but clouds.

The lower terminus of the Pilatus Bahn at Alpnachstad, just across the road from the Brünig line station and steamer pier.
(Martin Bairstow)

Approaching the summit. The most spectacular part of the route is a little further down where the line climbs on a ledge overlooking a sheer drop.
(Martin Bairstow)

Preserved at the Vehrkehrshaus in Luzern is No. 9, one of the original steam railcars of 1889.

(Martin Bairstow)

Conventional pointwork is impossible. A travolator gives access to the loop and the depot just above Alpnachstad station.

(Martin Bairstow)

Pointwork at the bottom end of the passing loop at Ämsigen.

(Martin Bairstow)

Bürgenstock

Sole public transport to the resort of Bürgenstock is afforded by the metre gauge funicular which climbs 440 metres in its length of 934 metres giving a maximum gradient of 580°/oo (steeper than 1 in 2).

The line opened on 8 July 1888, the first electrically operated funicular in Switzerland. In the early years, a rack rail, of the Abt variety, was laid between the running rails so as to provide a braking facility. This was discarded in 1910 by which time electrically driven funiculars were considered capable of having their speed controlled adequately through the winding gear.

The original rolling stock is still in use offering a seasonal service from April until October. The lower station at Kehrsiten – Bürgenstock is virtually on the steamer landing stage.

The Swiss Pass and Tell Pass are valid for free travel, the Swiss Card for half fare.

The funicular car descends to make its connection with our ship at Kehrsiten–Bürgenstock on 24 August 1995.
(Martin Bairstow)

Passing at the half way stage on the Bürgenstock Bahn.
(Martin Bairstow)

Stanserhorn

Opened on 23 August 1893, the Stanserhorn Bahn was the first Swiss funicular to manage without a rack rail for braking. With a length of almost 4 km, the line had to be divided into three independent sections: Stans – Kälti – Blumatt – Stanserhorn.

The first section, upon which the original rolling stock still operates, is 1,547 metres in length with a maximum gradient of 1 in 4.

The other two sections were steeper rising to almost 1 in 1$\frac{1}{2}$ but they were replaced by a cable car in 1974. This followed a fire in 1970 when lightning struck a cable destroying the 100 bed summit hotel and much of the funicular winding gear.

The combined funicular/cable car service operates from the middle of April until early November. The exact dates depend on the weather. The cable car is less susceptible to blockage by snow than were the upper sections of the old funicular.

The Swiss Pass and Swiss Card give a 25% reduction. The Tell Pass is valid for unlimited travel.

The lower terminus at Stans on 26 August 1994.
(Martin Bairstow)

The 1893 vintage rolling stock still runs on the first section to Kälti. *(Martin Bairstow)*

Looking down from the Stanserhorn: The funicular track abandoned in 1970, the replacement cable car and the Alpnachstad 'branch' of Vierwaldstättersee.
(Martin Bairstow)

Treib – Seelisberg

The village of Seelisberg is perched on the mountainside above the corner where Lake Luzern turns southwards by the Schiller Stein opposite Brunnen. Rail access has been available since 30 May 1916 when the metre gauge funicular opened from Treib. The line climbs 330 metres in a journey of 1134 metres, a maximum of 380°/oo or 1 in 2½.

An all year round service is provided with a basic ten trips each way in winter rising to as many as three an hour in summer, timed to connect with the ships at Treib.

Holders of Swiss Card and Swiss Pass pay half fare. The line is included on the Tell Pass.

Car No. 2 makes the ascent in June 1990.   *(Martin Bairstow)*

Car No. 1 is just visible inside Seelisberg station in August 1994.   *(Martin Bairstow)*

'The Stoos Express'

The ski resort and alpine village of Stoos stands 1290 metres above sea level.

Opened on 19 August 1933, the Stoos Bahn is a metre gauge funicular which climbs 703 metres from its lower station at Schlattli. With a maximum gradient of 781°/oo (1 in 1¼) it is the third steepest in Switzerland.

The line begins at a modest 1 in 4 crossing the Muota Torrent by a rather spectacular steel bridge which is difficult to photograph because of the trees. The gradient steepens gradually to the ruling 1 in 1¼. The line then passes through a 150 metre long tunnel before the half way passing loop. In the upper reaches it turns through nearly 90 degrees to reach the terminus at Stoos.

Schlattli has never been rail connected but is served by a bus to Schwyz Post (in the town centre). After a pause at Schwyz Post, this bus continues to Schwyz SBB station. Alternatively, there is a connection from Schwyz Post to Brunnen SBB or landing stage.

The line leaves Schlattli at 1 in 4 by a viaduct over the Muota Torrent. Then the climb really begins.
(Martin Bairstow)

Car No. 1 is close to the summit at Stoos on 27 August 1994.
(Martin Bairstow)

Schlattli station and viaduct.
(Martin Bairstow)

The upper terminus at Stoos. Just visible through the trees bottom left is the viaduct by which the funicular makes its very steep descent.
(Martin Bairstow)

The view from Stoos with Brunnen town and station in the distance and the lake top left.
(Martin Bairstow)

Vanished Attractions

With such a dense varied and almost universally modernised system still in full operation, one would not expect a very long chapter on the subject of closed lines. But there were some small enterprises which escaped modernisation.

Brunnen – Morschach – Axenstein

Dominating the skyline on the east side of Brunnen is the decaying ruin of the closed Grand Hotel. If we venture in this direction, past the end of the promenade to where the road begins to climb up, we can make out the lower terminus of the one time Brunnen – Morschach Bahn.

Opened on 1 August 1905 but closed on 29 March 1969, the line was just over 2 km in length. The gradient was 1 in 6 and the maximum speed just 9km per hour, the through journey taking 15 minutes.

Motive power came in the form of a small 0-4-0 locomotive onto which was articulated a carriage with two end compartments and an open saloon. An additional four wheel trailer could be added at the uphill end of the formation. Power supply was at 750 volts dc with two overhead wires. Pick up was by two trolley poles projecting from the locomotive. The gauge was metre with a Strub rack rail.

The ascent began through a tunnel but then there were excellent views over Lake Luzern as the line climbed towards Morschach, the limit of service in winter, then doubled back for the final attack on Axenstein.

Loco No. 3 propels its carriage into the tunnel just a short way distance above the Brunnen terminus in 1964. The railway had three of these locomotives, all built for the opening in 1905.
(Colin Mills)

Brunnen-Morschach-Axenstein-Bahn

Gültig **2 Tage**

Brunnen
Axenstein

B   Fr. **1.80**
B

01776

Gültig **10 Tage**

Brunnen
Morschach
und zurück

Fr **1.80**

B   T

03600

The Schwyz – Brunnen Tramway

The historic town of Schwyz lies some 2 km from the SBB station which is actually in the village of Seewen. From the opening of the Gotthard Line in 1882, a connection was provided by horse bus.

A concession was granted in 1890 for a standard gauge steam tramway but this was never built. Instead, a new concession was sought in 1898 for a metre gauge electric line.

Opened on 6 October 1900, the Strassenbahn Schwyz – Seewen was electrified at 750 volts three phase. The system was converted to 1,000 volts dc on 22 July 1914 in anticipation of the line being extended southward. The three existing trams were sold to Basel as trailers. They were replaced by six motor coaches and two trailers. There was also a trailer wagon for carrying the mail but later on this was replaced by a road vehicle on rubber tyres which was still coupled onto the tram.

The enterprise was now known as Schwyzer Strassenbahnen. The extension opened as far as Ibach on 12 October 1914 but the outbreak of the First World War curtailed tourist traffic and it was not considered worth running to Brunnen in winter. Service began to Brunnen on 8 May 1915 but was suspended again during the following winter after which the entire route operated all year round.

Just over 7 km in length, the line started at Schwyz SBB (then known as Seewen) at 455 metres above sea level. It climbed to 517 metres at Schwyz Post (town centre) then descended again passing Brunnen SBB before terminating at the steamer

One of the six motor coaches at Brunnen terminus in August 1953 in company with a bus of Auto AG Schwyz.
(Geoff Gamble)

terminal, 439 metres above sea level. The track was single and laid in the street until 1931 when a 2.5 km. section south of Ibach was rebuilt on roadside reservation. There were a total of 26 request stops en route.

The 1938 timetable shows 20 workings each way between Schwyz Post and Brunnen Schifflände. The service to Schwyz SBB operated separately but usually in connection. Frequency on this section was slightly greater to maximise main line connections.

The tramway closed on 15 December 1963 being replaced by the orange buses of Auto AG Schwyz.

On the roadside reservation near Ingenbohl.   *(Martin Bairstow collection)*

A Tour of Lake Zug

The motorship 'Zug' awaits departure from the town of Zug on 22 August 1994.   (Martin Bairstow)

Seasoned users of rover tickets will agree that, once you've bought the ticket, there is a temptation to try and get some value out of it and you are not over keen to spend time travelling on services outside the validity.

Maybe this is why I had not previously sampled a sail on Lake Zug. For some reason, this is the only big lake upon whose steamers the Swiss Pass is not valid for free travel. I presume that the same applies to other types of pass. You still get half fare but there will be a tendency for passholders to make fewer journeys on Lake Zug than they do on, say Luzern or Zürich.

I mention this because there may well be readers who are familiar with the Luzern ships but have never considered taking a sail on the neighbouring lake.

Service on Zugersee is less frequent. There are four trips each way May to October except on Sundays when the timetable is more comprehensive. The full journey from Zug to Arth am See takes about 90 minutes each way.

There are also a number of more specialised cruises. On three days a week in Summer, there is a lunch boat, a 1½ hour non landing cruise from Zug. On Wednesdays, Fridays and Saturdays right through the year there is a 'Kulinarische Abendrundfahrt' (gastronomic evening cruise) which takes either 2½ or 3 hours according to the menu. Such is the precision of the Swiss timetable, it actually spells out which dish gives which arrival time. Then every Sunday in Winter there is a 'Grosses-Winter-Brunch-Buffet' at 10.45 from Zug.

There are three ships, in order of size the 'Zug', 'Rigi' and 'Schwyz'. All have about half their carrying capacity in 'Bankettplätze' (banqueting seats) which tends to confirm that they are aiming at a slightly different market to the more cosmopolitan Lake Luzern.

Train and ship are no more than 600 metres apart at Zug, Cham, Oberwil and Walchwil but over 1km at Immensee. Arth am See is 3km from Arth Goldau. There used to be a tramway run by the Arth Rigi Bahn but this closed in 1959, the journey now being covered by bus.

Another local line which closed in 1959 was the tramway from Zug to Schönegg. Again this is replaced by a bus direct from Zug Station. At Schönegg we can change back onto the rail for the climb to Zugerberg. 1.2km in length, this funicular climbs at up to 480°/oo (almost 1 in 2) to Zugerberg (literally mountain of Zug) which is a village on a plateau and not just a summit. Because there is a resident population for whom the funicular is their staple public transport, the line is on the Swiss Pass as is the connecting bus. The combined service is shown in the funicular/cable car section of the timetable with a basic half hourly frequency Monday

Cham station with resident shunting engine looking towards Luzern on 22 August 1994. *(Martin Bairstow)*

Platform furniture and fahrdienstraum (effectively a signal box within the station building) at Cham. *(Martin Bairstow)*

A Zürich Flughafen (Airport) to Luzern express just east of Cham on 22 August 1994. The loco is propelling the push-pull formation. *(Martin Bairstow)*

to Fridays increased to every 20 minutes at weekends.

One can, of course, circumnavigate Lake Zug by main line train. Running the full length of the east bank is the main line from Zürich to the Gotthard. The 15 km between Zug and Arth Goldau are single track climbing at no more than 13°/oo (1 in 76) towards Arth Goldau. There is a good view of the lake most of the way. This section of line was opened by the Gotthard Bahn on 1 June 1897, the same day that the Nord Ost Bahn completed the direct route from Zürich to Zug. This is the route via the Zimmerberg and Albis Tunnels which we used for our journey from Zürich Airport.

The basic train service between Zug and Arth Goldau comprises an hourly express from Zürich which goes forward from Arth Goldau either fast to Italy or semi fast to Chiasso each alternate hour. The intermediate stations of Oberwil and Walchwil are served by local trains only in the early morning and late evening.

Zug Station stands on the junction between the lines from Zürich to Arth Goldau and to Luzern. There are platforms on the two diverging routes. The main building stands within the angle facing south. The first stretch of the Luzern line, running along the north shore of the lake, also dates from 1897. But from just east of Cham, as far as Rotkreuz it is part of the earlier line from Zürich to Luzern via Affoltern which opened in 1864. The junction east of Cham was removed in 1970 and trains from the Affoltern line now run into Zug by the loop line which takes them to the north end of the station.

The hourly train service between Zug and Luzern includes an express through from Zürich Airport and a local which calls at all stations.

The circuit of Lake Zug is completed between Rotkreuz and Arth Goldau by the original Gotthard main line, opened on 1 June 1882. This was widened from single to double track south of Immensee in 1904 but as late as 1963 between Rotkreuz and Immensee. The line climbs mostly at 1 in 100 all the way from Rotkreuz to Arth Goldau. It overlooks the lake as it makes its way along a ridge below the Rigi.

Passenger service over this section includes the hourly express from Luzern to the Gotthard, alternatively fast and semi fast, in opposite sequence to the hourly train from Zürich. There is the hourly Luzern to Flüelen stopping train which travels via Kussnacht joining the Lake Zug route at Immensee. Every two hours there is an express from Luzern to St Gallen. This also travels via and indeed stops at Kussnacht. On some workings this service introduces locos and carriages of the Sud Ost Bahn and the Bodensee Toggenburg. Finally, there is a local from Rotkreuz to Arth Goldau most hours but with some missing. This is through from Aarau via Lenzburg and Wohlen.

I finally made my tour of Lake Zug on Monday 22 August 1994. I travelled with Philippa and Stephen from Brunnen as far as Arth Goldau where they alighted for the Wild Life Park. I changed trains for Zug. Then it was the 10.45 ship which I took only as far as Cham paying half fare. I could have gone the full length to Arth am See but that pleasure had to be postponed till another time. The needs of this book suggested that I should do a bit of photography at Cham and then head towards Luzern and the Seetal line. During the course of the day, I reached Birrwil, Lenzburg and Zürich and was back in Zug at 4.32pm. I then took the bus to Schönegg for the ascent of the Zugerberg.

Immensee, where the line from Luzern via Kussnacht joins the route via Rotkreuz.   (Martin Bairstow)

The station building at Zug which stands in the angle between the Luzern line platforms (to the left) and those on the line to Arth Goldau. *(Martin Bairstow)*

Schönegg is the lower terminus of the Zugerberg funicular. The 'bendibus' covers the route of the pre 1959 tramway to Zug station. *(Martin Bairstow)*

Looking down on Lake Zug from the midpoint of the Zuberberg Bahn. *(Martin Bairstow)*

Das Verkehrshaus Der Schweiz
The Swiss Transport Museum

Opened on 1 July 1959, the museum occupies a site between the lake and the Luzern to Kussnacht railway. There is no station so access is either by trolleybus from Luzern or by steamer.

The railway section of the museum boasts more than 60 exhibits occupying over 1km of track. There is a working model of the Gotthard main line and driving simulator also based on a trip over the Gotthard.

On the shipping side, there is the original Rigi, the engine from the paddle steamer Pilatus together with models and videos depicting the story of transport on the Swiss lakes.

Other sections are devoted to road, cable and air transport, with a Swissair DC3 the largest exhibit.

The museum is open all year round from 9am until 6pm except from November to February when the hours are from 10 until 4. There is sufficient interest to occupy the best part of a day. There are refreshment facilities. We got a reduction on the entrance price with the guest card issued by our hotel in Brunnen.

4-2-0 No. 1 'Limmat' is a replica built 1947 of the loco which hauled the first train in Switzerland, from Zürich to Baden on 9 August 1847.
(Martin Bairstow)

Pioneer electric locomotives at the Vehrkehrshaus. Burgdorf Thun Bahn No. 2 was built in 1899 to inaugurate the first standard gauge electrification in Switzerland. Seebach–Wettingen No. 2 was built in 1904 for the first 15,000 volt a.c. scheme, the pioneer of what became the standard main line system in Switzerland, Germany and Austria.
(John Marshall)

Ein Ausflug (An excursion)

S G V
1/2 Preis
Gültig 1 Monat

Brunnen
Seelisberg
via Treib

2. Kl.   Fr 5.20

7002540

Our transport for part of the day, the 'Winkelried' pulling into Brunnen Pier. The village of Seelisberg is just visible above the main mast.
(Martin Bairstow)

Friday 26 August 1994. Our first objective is the Stanserhorn but we are a bit worried about the weather. Two days ago we set out on the same venture but, as our ship approached Beckenried, the heavens opened and the mountains were totally immersed in cloud so we stayed on board and went to the Vehrkehrshaus instead.

The shortest way from Brunnen to Stans is by steamer to Beckenried thence by postbus. Maybe we can attempt a slight variation as the postbus at 9.54 from Beckenreid actually starts from Seelisberg at 9.30 and we've never covered the bus journey between the two.

At 8.55 we are on Brunnen landing stage. The 'Winkelried' is circling round from its overnight berth at the Föhnhafen. There is a good crowd waiting to board including a large party of well equipped walkers. I suspect that they may be heading for Seelisberg. They cannot all fit on the funicular. Will this delay us? Would we be better staying on the 'Winkelried' to Beckenried?

We depart punctually at 9.00 and after six minutes are drawing towards the pier at Treib. The funicular 'driver', who still wears a traditional railway hat, is waiting to catch the rope thrown from the ship and then to help the crew manoeuvre the gangplank. He then retreats to his ticket office.

We are the first off the ship, through the turnstile by his ticket window and on to the funicular carriage. There is clearly some mobility of labour here. Another 'driver', complete with hat, is oiling the pulley wheels on the track just above the station.

9.10 departure time and still the walkers are filing off the boat. 9.13 and the warning bell sounds. The turnstile has evidently clocked up the maximum capacity of the funicular. The 'driver' closes the ticket office, walks up the stepped platform shutting

the sliding carriage doors and takes his position in the leading compartment. The remaining customers are left behind as we begin our ascent at a steady 10 km per hour.

As we climb higher we can see the 'Winkelried' crossing towards Gersau. At the halfway stage a virtually empty carriage passes on its way down. We must be consuming some electricity on this trip as our load is not counterbalanced!

As soon as we have all alighted, the bell goes again. The funicular is making an extra trip for the left behinds who will by now have boarded the other carriage at Treib.

Our postbus is standing outside the chalet style station. Evidently the driver had made the necessary enquiry at the station as he waits to see whether there are any customers amongst the rear party who soon begin to emerge.

We are away three minutes late at 9.33. The drive is certainly worth having made the extra change. A series of hairpin bends takes us back down to the lake level at Beckenried where there are a number of people waiting including, no doubt, some off the 'Winkelried' which will have left here 15 minutes ago.

A relief bus appears alongside. Our driver re-directs half the waiting customers in its direction. We proceed along the lakeside through Buochs and Ennetbürgen, both of which are served by a handful of steamers.

By this stage, both buses are full and standing. Suddenly there are a lot of police about in high visibility clothing. Then we encounter groups of soldiers in camouflage jackets. They can't both be correctly dressed but they are all on the same mission which soon becomes clear. There is an airshow at a military airfield in the flat strip of land which connects Ennetbürgen and Stans. There are

A descending car on the
Treib–Seelisberg funicular.
(Martin Bairstow)

The old station at Stansstad,
adjacent to the lake and
steamer terminal which was
abandoned when the line was
extended through to Luzern
in 1964.   *(Martin Bairstow)*

The newest ship in the fleet,
the 'Brunnen', built 1992, at
Alpnachstad on 26 August
1994.   *(Martin Bairstow)*

cars parked all over the showground but traffic on the road keeps moving. The police and army have evidently done a good job. Our bus half empties at the airshow.

We pull onto the station forecourt at Stans only a couple of minutes late. Soldiers attempt to give us airshow programmes and to direct us to special buses but we circumvent them. The timetable specifies a five minute walk to the Stanserhorn Bahn but which direction? Fortunately there is a map of Stans on the wall. We are held up at a level crossing by the departing 10.25 to Luzern. Will we make our 10.30? No problem. Once over the crossing, the funicular is straight ahead of us. We show our tickets and board the 101 year old carriage.

The 'driver' shuts the doors, climbs on board and gives the starting signal from a small console on the platform adjacent to his position — no high tech equipment on board this vehicle.

We trundle up to Kätli to complete the first stage of the journey. Prior to 1970, we would have reached the summit by two similar funicular sections. Instead we change on to the cable car. This may be quicker and less susceptible to blockage by snow but it is not comfortable.

Everybody on the funicular had occupied a seat. Now they crowd on to the cable car which only has six seats. Everyone else becomes a 'strap hanger' (which is, I believe, a New York term to describe a subway commuter). The car swings a little after crossing each pylon but otherwise the ride is very smooth. Down below we can see the overgrown funicular track including the intermediate station at Blumatt. You can still alight here on request if you don't mind climbing down the pylon from the cable car.

The hope when reaching the summit is that it will be a clear day. We are fairly lucky. There are clouds but the view is clear in all directions most of the time. The paddle steamer 'Unterwalden' is making its way from Stansstad over to Hergiswil en route from Luzern to Alpnachstad.

There is a 90 minute gap in the Stanserhorn service after 11.45. We could have lunch here but decide instead to try a second ascent of the Pilatus. After all it may be a long time before we have another Tell Pass. We go down on the 11.45 which only has six passengers so we all get a seat on the cable car and a compartment to ourselves on the funicular.

We join the 12.25 Luzern train at Stans, a very well appointed LSE coach. No time to get our lunch out however as we are only on four minutes to Stansstad. We've done this change before but I check the timetable to remind myself that it is only 500 metres from train to ship. We should do that easily in 11 minutes.

It would hardly have been necessary to walk at all if Stansstad Station were still in its pre 1964 position adjacent to the lakeside. The station building is there at right angles to the lake but long out of railway use.

Approaching the pier is the 'Brunnen', the newest ship in the fleet. It leaves at 12.40 sailing direct to Alpnachstad in 20 minutes, just enough time to butter some rolls and have a bite of lunch.

The Pilatus crowds will have gone up in the morning but the two carriages in the platform are still pretty full. A driver directs us to wait on the platform, which takes the form of a flight of steps, as he goes over to the bottom most car standing on the other track. The first loaded car sets off 3 minutes early with the other close behind. A third then drops down to the bottom, comes across the travolator and moves up to the platform. We board and depart on time at 1.10.

The carriage resembles a funicular car, with compartments in step formation. As soon as it moves the sensation is clearly that of a rack railway with the slight vibration caused by the grinding of the pinion wheels on the rack.

We climb steeply through woodlands. The stone viaduct across the Wolfort ravine then the short Wolfort Tunnel bring us on to the slopes of the Risleten. After a number of further short tunnels, we arrive at Ämsigen, the half way point which is a passing place but not a station.

There can be as many as five ascending and descending cars which must all pass here. Today there are three going up and two coming down. The drivers of the rear cars in each direction telephone to report that they are clear of the points at the entrance to the loop. Then the points slide over and soon we are off again.

It is the final stages of the journey that the most dramatic scenery is encountered. From our position in the third ascending coach, we can see the other two cars winding their way towards the summit, a discreet distance apart. Between short tunnels, the line is carried on a shelf blasted out of the limestone wall of the Esel. At one point the track passes over a sheer precipice. Finally the summit hotel comes into view.

There are three platforms, each comprising a flight of steps and each capable of holding two carriages. It is everyday practice to have cars standing at the summit during the day because the peak flow is upwards in the morning and downward later in the day.

Just below the station, there is a siding, accessible only from the top end, which can accommodate carriages waiting between turns. It looks so odd for a siding on a gradient of 1 in 2½ not to have a buffer stop at the bottom end. On reflection, it is perhaps most reassuring to know that one is not considered necessary.

Tonight there is to be an open air concert and trains are to run later than the normal 21.45 last service. Let us hope that the weather improves for them. I try to photograph the next arrival at 14.20. Just one car this time. The clouds are rising faster than the train. By the time it gets close enough, it is invisible.

The car in front winding its way along and through the wall of the Esel towards the summit of Pilatus.
(Martin Bairstow)

This is the risk you take when you invest in a ticket to one of the mountain summits. We're not too disappointed as this is our second ascent. We return on the 14.25 to Alpnachstad where we have 25 minutes to wait for the 15.30 to Luzern.

This is a push-pull set – a recent innovation on the local service between Giswil and Luzern. The locomotive at the rear is anything but new. The Brünig line was electrified during the Second World War as an emergency but the 1941 built locomotives were clearly intended to last.

Philippa and Stephen express a preference to return to Brunnen for a swim. They could take the 16.27 local from Luzern direct but settle for the 16.19 Eurocity 'Tiziano' changing at Arth Goldau. Apparently Stephen set the alarm going in the DB toilet much to Philippa's embarrassment.

I have my eyes set on one more summit. I board the 'Pilatus' leaving Luzern at 16.10 for Kehrsiten – Bürgenstock. Behind us in pier No. 1, the 'Uri' is preparing to depart at 16.15 non-stop to Vitznau.

We call at the Vehrkehrshaus allowing the 'Uri' to catch up. The two ships then run side by side, the 'Uri' gradually getting ahead and cutting in front of us. We follow in its wake only letting it go as we turn into our Hertenstein stop. Business done here, we cross the lake to Kehrsiten – Bürgenstock. The timetable shows this as the shortest distance of all between train and ship – 20 metres. I have eight minutes in which to cover this distance.

The carriage of the Bürgenstock Bahn carries a motif recording the centenary of the line 1888-1988. This is another vintage funicular – and a steep one. As we approach the summit, I remember why I obtained no photograph of it on an earlier trip in 1990. There is simply no vantage point at the summit from which you can see the line.

You can however see most other things. 'Dass ist Zugersee' says a man to his small child pointing to a distant lake beyond Luzern. I cannot resist the temptation to correct this child's education pointing out that Lake Zug is visible beyond the Kussnacht arm of Lake Luzern and that what he is looking at is Baldeggersee in the Seetal. The man apologises that as a Swiss person he has never been here before, asks me where I come from, congratulates me on my German and generally boosts my ego.

I wander back to the funicular and take a standing position on the front platform which appears to be the most popular place on the carriage. The driver comes along and says that he doesn't mind how many people wish to travel here as long as they leave room for him.

It is 17.35 and a ship is tying up at the landing stage 445 metres below. It is the 'Brunnen' on the 16.35 'all stations' from Alpnachstad to Luzern. Away in the distance, our own transport home, the 'Winkelried' is just pulling away from its stop at the Vehrkehrshaus.

The descent begins at 17.40. I could have had a

110-005 (ex 905) pauses at Alpnachstad on the Luzern to Giswil push-pull waiting to cross the corresponding working the other way.
(Martin Bairstow)

The Pilatus restarts from Kehrsiten–Bürgenstock on its journey to Alpnachstad.
(Martin Bairstow)

The Bürgenstock funicular awaits custom from the next steamer connection.
(Martin Bairstow)

seat further back but the view is better from here. I manage to photograph the ascending carriage at the half way stage. Arrival at Kehrsiten is at 17.47 leaving just 10 minutes to wait for the 'Winkelried'. The funicular driver takes the opportunity to polish his carriage windows in readiness for his next departure at 18.00.

The 'Winkelried' arrives. A wedding party, complete with bride in white regalia, alight from the first class and change onto the century old funicular. I am reminded of our own wedding earlier in 1994 when Philippa and I had to squeeze on to a rush hour Class 155 at Leeds.

The lake steamer is an everyday workhorse as much as it is a tourist attraction. A cart load of 'fly luggage' is unloaded at Weggis.

The light is getting awful and Philippa has taken the camera with the higher speed film. Just after leaving Vitznau, we pass the paddle steamer 'Gallia'. I position myself for a photograph but can get a reading no faster than 1/30 second. Suddenly I can see two 'Gallias' through my viewfinder: the real one to the left and a reflection of the white ship against the very dull background in the glass to my right. It might be an atmospheric shot. But will it be any good at 1/30 second? I hesitate a moment too long so we will never know the answer.

I retire inside to write up my notes. There is just one more connection in which I am interested. The 'Winkelried' is due into Brunnen at 19.47. Evening meal is until 20.00 but is that the last time for going in or the time by which we should be out? I can save ten minutes by changing onto a bus at Gersau. There are only two minutes there but the timetable actually specifies one minute as the required interval for a connection at Gersau.

I don't know where the bus stop is but it must be close. The ship arrives punctually at 19.25. The bus for Brunnen and Schwyz is waiting not five metres away directly outside the pier building. At 19.26, the connecting SGV bus arrives from Kussnacht and at 19.27 we depart.

The bus drives along the shore road. After a couple of minutes we overtake the 'Winkelried' now half way to Treib. Across on the hillside, the Seelisberg funicular is coming down to meet it. Bus travel can be quite agreeable in these circumstances.

I am not on for long. At 19.37 I am back in Brunnen after a trip of 10 hours 37 minutes. It has involved 17 different journeys: four by ship, five by funicular, and two each by bus, cable car, rack railway and 'normal' metre gauge train. Punctuality and reliability have been as near 100% as one could ever wish.

The trip has involved both a Swiss Pass and a Tell Pass – an extravagance justified only by the demands of writing this book. Had we had Swiss Pass only, it is likely that we would have covered only one of the Stanserhorn or Pilatus paying the appropriate reduced fare. We would have had to pay half fare on the Treib – Seelisberg Bahn and on the Gersau to Brunnen bus though these could have been avoided by staying longer on the steamer.

Had we had Tell Pass only, then it would have cost half fare on the postbus and also on the SBB though that could have been avoided in favour of travelling by ship albeit at the expense of Philippa's swim.

Most of the foregoing was actually written on the day of the trip in blissful ignorance of the scale of the traffic created by 'Air 94', the display put on by the army near Buochs.

Over that weekend, the SBB and LSE made provision for the extra business. At peak times there was a service every 15 minutes between Luzern and Stansstad provided by a combination of normal and extra trains. The hourly Luzern – Engelberg was strengthened up to 12 coaches (four LSE 3 coach sets) as far as Stansstad. Additional trains were made up of 12 Brünig Line carriages with a locomotive at each end. Postbuses were then provided from Stansstad to the airfield.

On the Saturday, some 22,000 customers were dealt with. According to *Schweizer Eisenbahn Review* (October 1994), the trains kept time but, towards the end of the day, the connecting buses became stuck in traffic and could not get to Stansstad. They were diverted to Stans Station where the LSE mobilised its 'last reserves' using a two coach formation to convey people to the longer trains waiting at Stansstad.

The 'Schiffstation' at Gersau blends well into the picturesque lakeside village.
(Martin Bairstow)

An early poster showing a funicular car near the upper terminus of the Stanserhorn Bahn which was destroyed by fire in 1970.

The 1892 service on the Pilatus Bahn. These 'period piece' posters are back in vogue. This one was on display at the summit in 1994.

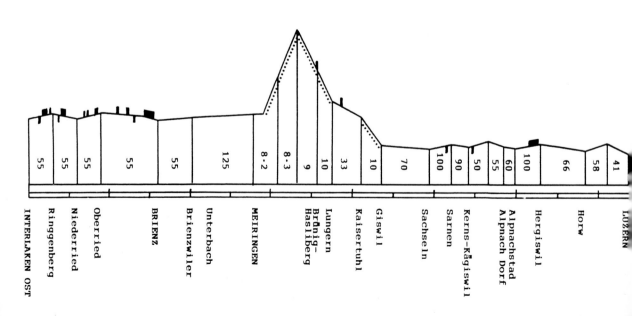

INTERLAKEN OST · Ringgenberg · Niederried · Oberried · BRIENZ · Brienzwiler · Unterbach · MEIRINGEN · Brünig-Hasliberg · Lungern · Kaisertuhl · Giswil · Sachseln · Sarnen · Kerns-Kägiswil · Alpnachstad Alpnach Dorf · Hergiswil · Horw · LUZERN

55 · 55 · 55 · 55 · 55 · 125 · 8·2 · 8·3 · 9 · 10 · 33 · 10 · 70 · 100 · 90 · 50 · 55 · 60 · 100 · 66 · 58 · 41

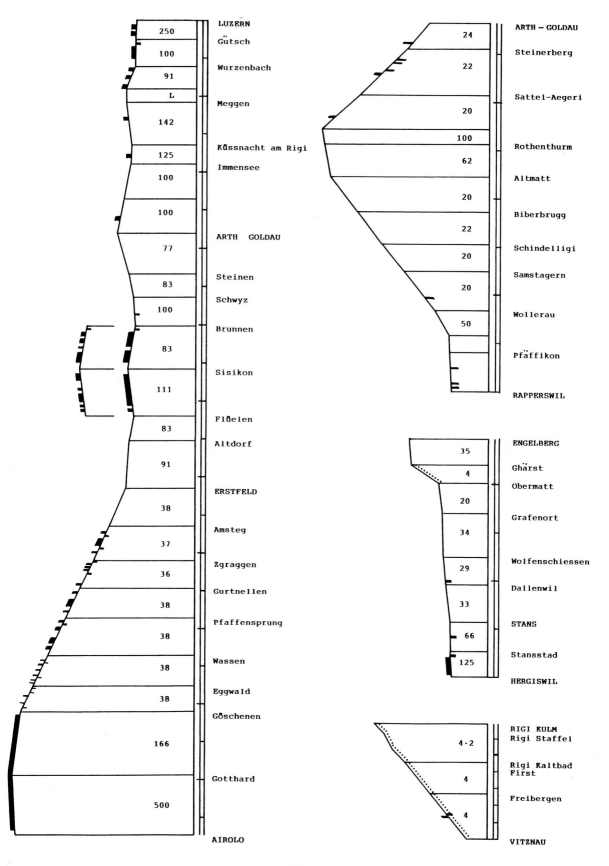

LUZERN
250
Gütsch
100
Wurzenbach
91
L
Meggen
142
Küssnacht am Rigi
125
Immensee
100
100
ARTH GOLDAU
77
Steinen
83
Schwyz
100
Brunnen
83
Sisikon
111
Flüelen
83
Altdorf
91
ERSTFELD
38
Amsteg
37
Zgraggen
36
Gurtnellen
38
Pfaffensprung
38
Wassen
38
Eggwald
38
Göschenen
166
Gotthard
500
AIROLO

24
ARTH – GOLDAU
Steinerberg
22
Sattel-Aegeri
20
100
Rothenthurm
62
Altmatt
20
Biberbrugg
22
Schindelligi
20
Samstagern
20
Wollerau
50
Pfäffikon
RAPPERSWIL

35
ENGELBERG
Ghärst
4
Obermatt
20
Grafenort
34
Wolfenschiessen
29
Dallenwil
33
STANS
66
Stansstad
125
HERGISWIL

RIGI KULM
Rigi Staffel
4·2
Rigi Kaltbad
First
4
Freibergen
4
VITZNAU

Appendix

Gotthard Main Line
(standard gauge)

opened

1	6	1864	Luzern - Cham
1	1	1882	Göschenen - Airolo
1	6	1882	Rotkreuz - Göschenen
1	6	1897	Luzern - Immensee
1	6	1897	Thalwil - Arth Goldau
1	6	1897	Cham - Zug

electrified (15,000 volts a.c.)

13	9	1920	Göschenen - Airolo
18	10	1920	Erstfeld - Göschenen
1	5	1922	Arth Goldau - Erstfeld
28	5	1922	Luzern - Arth Goldau
22	6	1922	Zug - Arth Goldau
6	7	1922	Rotkreuz - Immensee
9	10	1922	Luzern - Zug
5	2	1923	Thalwil - Zug

Sud Ost Bahn
(standard gauge)

opened

1	5	1877	Wädenswil - Einsiedeln
27	8	1878	Rapperswil - Pfäffikon
8	8	1891	Biberbrugg - Arth Goldau
8	8	1891	Samstagern - Pfäffikon

electrified (15,000 volts a.c.)

15	5	1939	throughout

Seetalbahn
(standard gauge)

opened

1	6	1859	Luzern - Emmenbrücke
3	9	1883	Emmenbrücke - Beinwil
15	10	1883	Beinwil - Lenzburg
23	1	1887	Beinwil - Menziken
1	10	1906	Menziken - Beromünster

electrified (5,500 volts a.c.)

10	5	1910	Beromünster - Lenzburg
11	7	1910	Hochdorf - Beinwil
1	10	1910	Emmenbrücke - Hochdorf

electrified (15,000 volts a.c.)

23	2	1924	Luzern - Emmenbrücke
1	10	1930	Emmenbrücke - Lenzburg
1	10	1930	Beinwil - Beromünster

closed to passeners

30	5	1992	Beinwil - Beromünster

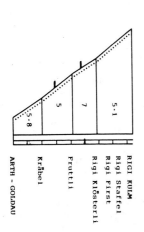

Rigi Bahnen
(standard gauge)

opened

23	5	1871	Vitznau - Staffelhöhe
27	6	1873	Staffelhöhe - Rigi Kulm
4	6	1875	Arth am See - Staffel

electrified (540 volts d.c.)

1	1	1906	Arth am See - Arth Goldau

electrified (1,500 volts d.c.)

20	5	1907	Arth Goldau - Rigi Kulm
3	10	1937	Vitznau - Staffel

closed

31	8	1959	Arth am See - Arth Goldau

Brünig Line
(metre gauge)

opened

14	6	1888	Alpnachstad - Brienz
1	6	1889	Luzern - Alpnachstad
23	8	1916	Brienz - Interlaken Ost

electrified (15,000 volts a.c.)

18	11	1941	Luzern - Meiringen
24	12	1942	Meiringen - Interlaken Ost

Luzern - Stans - Engelberg
(metre gauge)

opened

5	10	1898	Stansstad - Engelberg
19	12	1964	Hergiswil - Stansstad

electrified (750 volts 3 phase)

5	10	1898	Stansstad - Engelberg

electrified (15,000 volts a.c.)

19	12	1964	Hergiswil - Engelberg

Pilatus
(80cm gauge)

opened

4	6	1889	Alpnachstad - Pilatus

electrified (1,550 volts d.c.)

15	5	1937	Alpnachstad - Pilatus

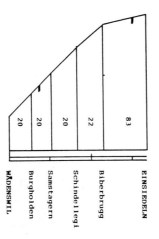

Bürgenstock
(metre gauge funicular)

opened

8	7	1888	Kehrsiten - Bürgenstock

Stanserhorn
(metre gauge funicular)

opened

23	8	1893	Stans - Stanserhorn

closed

1	9	1974	Kälti - Stanserhorn

Seelisberg
(metre gauge funicular)

opened

30	5	1916	Trieb - Seelisberg

Stoosbahn
(metre gauge funicular)

opened

19	8	1933	Schlattli - Stoos

Zugerberg
(metre gauge)

opened

20	3	1907	Zug - Schönegg

(electrified 550 volts d.c.)

14	5	1907	Schönegg - Zugerberg (funicular)

closed

10	5	1959	Zug - Schönegg

Schwyzer Strassenbahn
(metre gauge)

opened

6	10	1900	Schwyz SBB - Schwyz Post
12	10	1914	Schwyz Post - Ibach
8	5	1915	Ibach - Brunnen

electrified (750 volts 3 phase)

6	10	1900	Schwyz SBB - Schwyz Post

electrified (1,000 volts d.c.)

22	7	1914	Schwyz SBB - Schwyz Post
12	10	1914	Schwyz Post - Ibach
8	5	1915	Ibach - Brunnen

closed

15	12	1963	Schwyz SBB - Brunnen

Brunnen - Axenstein (metre gauge)

1	8	1905	opened
29	3	1969	closed

electrified (740 volts d.c.)